THE THROW AWAY GIRL

A MEMOIR

TIFFANY BARNES

Paperback Edition 2023

Published by Flame Within Press

Original Copyright @2023

By Tiffany Barnes

This is an account of real-life events that may be triggering as they touch upon topics of sexual, physical, and emotional abuse.

Some names have been changed within the story to protect the safety and privacy of all parties involved.

Cover Design by Jennie Stevens

Published in the United States of America

BISAC

Memoir, Nonfiction

ISBN

EBOOK 979-8-9872962-0-2

PAPERBACK 979-8-9872962-1-9

This book is dedicated to my fellow survivors:
Speak your truth even if your voice shakes. You're not alone. It's not
your fault. I see you. Keep on shining your light!

the beginning

FROM THE OUTSIDE, MY childhood appeared perfectly normal. We lived in a small 500 sq ft, one-bedroom house in a quiet town outside of Salt Lake City, UT called Layton. Most houses around us seemed more updated than ours, but the world around our place was big and the perfect escape filled with wonder. Our neighbors had paved driveways and nice lawns, while we had a dirt driveway and a yard filled with bushes, trees, and old cars.

Our home was on a busy, main street but the community had its sense of safety in what felt like country living to me. We had open land wrapped around our house with apricot, peach and plum trees, and two old wooden sheds on each side of the chicken coop. An irrigation ditch ran on the side and front of our house, and some of Dad's old cars sat on the lot. His favorite one was his 1964 Chevy Bel-air. I spent hours outside making mud pies, hiding in the old sheds, and eating from the grapevines and plum trees. We had tall lilac bushes that lined the dirt driveway, and when it came time for blooming season, the aroma was an empowering sweet blend of freshness, and a dash of honey. Seeing the purple petals pop from each bud delighted me.

Purple was my favorite color.

I loved building tree houses and climbing trees. That was my escape. My favorite tree was over 100 years old, and it stood right by the sheds in front of the grapevines. Out of all the trees we had, it was the biggest. I'd find scrap pieces of wood and haul them up the tree to make a seat so that I could have a bird's eye view. Looking down from where I sat, I was safe, and everything appeared so big and expansive. I kept a lookout on our family and street, and no one could see me.

The trees held sanctuary. Yet, inside our house, something was wrong. Beyond the façade, I lived a life of abuse. The physical beatings weren't as painful as the emotional and mental trauma that I had endured.

Every Sunday, we'd put on our best clothes and go to church like many Utahns did.

Dad worked long hours to support us and was saving up money to buy us a home one day. Mom hardly worked at all. Now and then, she'd pick up a job at McDonald's or another fast-food restaurant, but it never lasted.

"What happened, Mom?" I'd ask. "Why are you home early?"

She cursed and then yelled about how she was wrongly accused of something she didn't do, and then she'd leave to go to her room, slamming the door.

Mom and Dad used the only bedroom in the house, and my "bedroom" was in the kitchen. My twin bed was pushed up against the wall to make room for the kitchen table. When walking into the 100-200 sq. ft. room, you'd immediately bump into my bed. The sink and counter were on the left, and the refrigerator was on my right. I could almost touch my hand to the fridge while I laid in bed. The house didn't have central heating. We had a heater located in the wall that went from the floor to the ceiling, and my pillow was two feet from it, which was nice and warm in the winter. My cardboard toy box got tucked in behind the door. It was tight but cozy.

When I'd come home from kindergarten, Mom would be watching her daytime soaps, either Charles in Charge or General Hospital— the show where she got my name from. Mom spent her time eating junk food while watching her shows. Her regular snacks of choice were beef jerky, chili cheese Fritos, Funyuns, pickles, cookies, and candies.

I licked my lips and asked if I could have some too.

"Can't you see I'm watching a show?" She sneered at me and then changed her facial expression to a smirk. "Oh. You want one?" Mom asked, waving the treat around like I was a circus animal.

I nodded. They all looked good to me.

Mom glared at me and quickly took the snack away from my reach. "You don't deserve one. They're all for me," she said.

I sunk to the ground and held my knees. Mom never shared. I wanted to be seen and close to her, but I felt like she only wanted to throw me away. Dad's favorite treat was Twix and caramels. He liked to keep his plastic-wrapped square caramels in a special cookie tin. *His* special cookie tin.

Mom had asked if I wanted a caramel from the tin one day while dad was at work. I agreed with delight, and we both ate one together. I really liked connecting with Mom and having her share special treats with me.

When Dad came home that night, I tensed my shoulders and laid quietly in my bed. I was half-asleep. Mom watched her usual night show, "Hogan's Heroes," in the living room like she did every night.

"Guess who got into your caramels today?" Mom said.

I held my breath and pretended to be asleep, knowing what was coming.

Why did she say that? She was the one who gave it to me.
Doesn't she care about me?

Stomping came toward my direction, and the sound of the cookie tin clattered against the floor. The blanket wrapped on me slid to the floor, and Dad yanked me out of bed.

I never fought back.

The bridge on my nose burned and ached, and everything else was a blur. I'm not sure how I got to bed or how long the beating occurred, but the stinging sensation in my nose stuck with me that night.

On a different evening, I got up in the middle of the night as my stomach grumbled from hunger. The house was too quiet. I clenched my fingers and called out for my parents, but no one answered.

Maybe they're outside?

"Mom? Dad?" I yelled.

Still no response.

I walked to the small window on our back door and gazed outside. The trees weren't my welcoming sanctuary at night. They were vast, unknown, and a place where things could lurk in the darkness. I shivered and looked away.

Is Dad's truck here?

I peered back up through the window and noticed what I had already felt. Dad's truck wasn't in the driveway, and I was alone in the house.

Where did they go?

Did they abandon and leave me?

I was five years old, all alone in the dark, and left to my devices in our tiny house. My hands started to shake, and my stomach growled. I'm scared and hungry. I moved toward the fridge and began searching for something to eat.

Where are those snacks I see mom eating all the time?

I kept rummaging. The best thing I found was a bottle of A-1 steak sauce. I took it out of the fridge, sat on the kitchen floor, and drank the sauce straight from the bottle. It was good, satisfying, and salty.

Mom and Dad walk through the door. At the sight of me on the floor in front of the fridge they begin yelling and questioning. "Why are you awake? You've made a mess!"

I was confused about why they were mad at me for taking care of myself when they left me. I was hungry.

Everything I did seemed to be a burden or a problem to Mom. I felt shame for being an inconvenience and needing support, and I never quite measured up for her. Even when I tried my hardest to be good, it still ended up being a failure or a conflict. I *just* wanted to sit on the couch together and watch a show with Mom while we ate *her* favorite snacks. I *just* wanted to have a project from school be approved or celebrated by her, but instead, she was spending time with another man, watching her shows, or we were at Grammie's house. I never complained about going to Grammie's house though. I loved spending time with her. I wanted to be seen, loved, and noticed in a good light, and with Grammie, I was.

On my sixth birthday, Grammie was there in the morning to greet me. She hummed and moved around like she had a happy secret to share.

I wonder what she's excited about?

"Guess what?" She smiled.

"It's my birthday!"

"Indeed, it is. Guess what else?"

I shrugged. It's my birthday. What else is there?

"You have a baby brother," she said. "Isn't that wonderful?"

No. Not today.

He was supposed to be born the day before, but instead arrived at 12:55 am on my day of my celebration. I wanted that to be MY special day.

Just for ME.

It was the one day of the year that I felt truly special and seen, and now it was given to my brother, too? I wasn't happy about it, but I also worried if he was going to be hit, like I was.

How will this change things for me?

Will having a new baby be good or bad thing?

How will I protect us both?

Shortly after Trent was born, something much darker took over mom that I couldn't explain or understand. Mom was behind closed doors in her bedroom with one of the men who came over during the day while Dad was at work. I sat in the living room working on my learning books when Trent started crying in his crib. The bottle in his crib was empty. I put my crayon down and stared at Mom's bedroom door, waiting for her to respond to him.

Mom, are you coming?

I felt terrible my brother was so upset and that there wasn't anyone else to take care of him.

He needs me.

"It's okay, buddy." I patted his head and grabbed the bottle before moving into the kitchen. I got up on the counter to rinse it and placed the formula powder inside and I leaned toward the sink to fill it with water. Mom emerged from the bedroom, wrapped in her robe. She stared at the crying baby and redirected her sight on the bottle in my hand.

Her eyes filled with fury. "Why did you take your brother's bottle?!"

I looked at her with confusion and before I could explain myself, she smacked the bottle out of my hand. Mom grabbed a butter knife from the kitchen counter and swung it at me. I didn't have time to move or tell her I was trying to take care of the baby she ignored. The butter knife sliced my scalp.

I cried out in pain and shock.

"Oh shit," Mom hustled me into the bathroom.

There was some blood, and it got into my eyes. I waited for her to comfort me. She didn't hug me, rub my back, or say soothing words to make it better.

Instead, she hastily picked me up and carried me into the bathroom, setting me down on the toilet.

She stared at me. "Stop crying and be quiet."

I nodded, and she left to get the neighbor, who was a registered nurse. The neighbor came over, and mom told her that I'd slipped and fallen, cutting my head open.

I said nothing.

I didn't want mom to hit me again.

With the neighbor's help, she cleaned me up, put a butterfly bandage on my head to stop the bleeding, and returned home.

"If you tell Dad what happened, I'll break your face." Mom reminded me like she had many times before.

When Dad returned from work, he noticed the bandage on my head. He asked Mom, "What happened to Tiffany today?" She fed him the same lie she told the neighbor and I kept quiet as I promised.

Please let this end.

I hoped that things would change, but the abuse continued. I slowly began to live in fear in my own house, as I'm alone with Mom most of the day. The slightest offense is met with violent punishment. If I ate the French fries she left out, I got a beating with dad's leather belt. Once, I peed and pooped in the water while she gave me a rare bath. I'm frightened to say anything about needing to get out of the tub to go to the bathroom because of what might happen; she beat me anyways. Mom hit me over the head with my favorite toy, a magic baton. The baton cracked in two, now it's ruined.

One time, the school nurse called mom to come pick me up after I threw up in class. Mom never showed up.

At times, she dragged me around by my hair, ripping out large clumps with her bare hands. Mom told me that if she knew I would be her child, she would've had an abortion. I'm also reminded that if she could, she would've "thrown me away."

Going to school meant no longer being stuck in the house with mom all day which was nice, but school presents its own set of problems. I'm often not bathed for days at a time, and I go to school dirty and unwashed. I wore old beat-up clothes that my parents would get at second-hand stores. At school, the other kids teased me because of my appearance. One day, I'm beaten up by another girl in the bathroom. She grabbed my earring and ripped it out of my ear. I held my ear and sobbed as the pain was overwhelming, and she continued to hit me. I clung to my bleeding ear, crouched down, and got away. Mom was called into the principal's office to meet with the girl's parents. She didn't defend me; instead, she spewed racial slurs at the girl and her mother. They were African American.

The yelling continued as mom lashed out at everyone in the room.

She didn't talk with them to figure things out or find ways to calm herself down.

Why is she behaving like this?

Nothing got solved, and we're escorted out of the principals' office.

Great, yet ANOTHER thing for kids to make fun of while I'm at school.

It still was better than home.

I'm scared at home. I spent more and more time outside, climbing trees, and I sat high up in the branches, feeling the wind and air. I dreamed of being far away from there. As I escaped up in the trees, my mind wandered for hours, but eventually, I *had* to go back into the house. Often, I dreamed of driving away to Grammie's house. It was fun there. More importantly, it was safe there. She was mom's mother—yet she couldn't be more different—Grammie was full of life, love, and compassion. We made pies together. She let me roll out the dough with her and braided my hair. Grammie wrote beautiful poetry. She tickled my back and acted silly with me by making funny faces and doing the robot. Grammie got a kick out of seeing us jump and waited for just the right moment to scare us unexpectedly. We made art out of everyday things. Regular bottle glass became something beautiful in her hands. I was mesmerized watching her create. She helped me believe that life could be BEAUTIFUL. Most of all, she always told me she loved me and found multiple ways to make me feel so loved.

My cousins came over to Grammie's. A place where we built blanket forts, swung on the swing set, went to the park down the street, and played for hours. We pretended we were pirates searching for buried treasure, and we formed a secret society of treasure hunters called club DRI.

Grammie's house was a refuge. It's the only place I got to be and feel like a normal kid. She tried to help when she saw Mom hit me. Mom didn't try to hide it and she did it right in front of my Grammie.

Grammie would pull Mom aside to talk to her privately, but she didn't listen. Mom was so fixated on yelling and unleashing her rage on those around her with her cunning words, that she didn't see anything else. She was intense. Grammie got the brunt of it and eventually, she gave up, left in tears from being beaten down and intimidated by Mom.

Dad saw none of Mom's abusive behavior. His love for her blinded him. We didn't have much money, but he gave Mom a portion from every paycheck to spend on herself. He paid for her to get her hair dyed each month. It was always a different color. She used the money to buy blouses or Avon products from a catalog and pranced around in new fashionable clothes while I sulk in shame, still in my second-hand clothing from the thrift store.

One evening, Mom told Dad that I stole gum at the store and needed to be punished for what I did. I have no idea what she's saying. I did no such thing. Dad seemed to believe pretty much whatever Mom said to him.

Why is she lying about me to him, again?

I closed my eyes tighter.

Maybe it is all just a bad dream?

I'm suddenly shaken awake. Before I know what's going on, Dad struck me across the nose. My head shivered with shock.

I'm dazed.

My nose bled.

Why's dad hitting me?

Why does he believe her?

I didn't do anything.

Why's Mom making things up?

My head was in a rush of pain and confusion. Dad hit me again, knocking the air out of me, and I grabbed my chest, trying to take a breath. He left me to nurse my wounds alone in the dark kitchen that I called a bedroom.

These late-night punishments became a pattern. His love twisted him to see things that weren't there. I paid the cost of this twisting.

None of it made sense.

Why would a mother do such a thing?

Yet, she did. The punishments continued, and I ended up with a broken rib, arm, and collarbone. There were times when Dad beat me for no reason whatsoever. When he was mad with Mom, he took it out on me.

I was an easy target.

CHAPTER TWO

broken

ONE AFTERNOON, I SAT on the floor in the living room, drawing in my coloring book. I tried to distract myself from the arguing happening with Mom and Dad in their bedroom.

This is not going to end well for me.

I looked around for a place to hide, but our home was too small to disappear anywhere. I clung tighter to the purple crayon I held and focused on the picture in front of me.

It felt like a long while of doodling until Dad madly swung the bedroom door open and Mom followed him. I stiffened. Without a word, he jerked me to my feet and threw me across the room. The right side of my body hit hard against our wooden front door.

Why's Dad doing this?

Why's Mom not helping me?

Pain shot up and down my arm. I couldn't stop crying as I laid on the ground at the front door. Dad stared wide-eyed but didn't move, and Mom stood in the doorway.

Do I get up?

Why isn't someone coming to see if I'm okay?

The pain was intense but moving wasn't something I wanted to do. I wondered if I laid still enough, maybe I could camouflage into the ground away from this space of fear. Mom unfroze from her spot and followed behind him as he paced.

"Talk to me. Talk to me," Mom yelled.

"I need to go to work," Dad barked and shoved past her.

Mom responded by demanding Dad to take us to Grammie's house. It was on the same route. She didn't appear to care that I was on the ground, just that she had somewhere to be.

We're going to see Grammie!

I needed her and we were on our way. That motivated me enough to pick myself up off the ground.

My arm continued to throb, but yet, I felt dazed. I somehow got in the car, and I heard Mom and Dad continuing to argue as we drove, but it sounded muffled in my zoned state. I nursed my arm and tried to focus on something other than the pain and the fighting, but both were too intense.

Were they fighting about my arm?

What did I do wrong?

Please stop the pain. Grammie.

We pulled up in front of her house. The seat belt strapped across me was strong and heavy, and it pressed against my arm, pinning me down, making my arm hurt even more. I tried to undo the seat belt, but I couldn't move my wrist. Dad yelled at me to undo the seat belt, so he was not late for work. With tears rolling down my face, I took a deep breath.

"I can't do it." I stared down at the floor.

"Fine," he hollered. Dad pressed down on the seatbelt and yanked me out of the truck, handing me off to mom. Without looking back, Dad drove away, and Mom and I walked into Grammie's house. All I could think about as I stood in the kitchen was how much my arm hurt. Tears welled up in my eyes as Grammie came toward me. She glanced at me, patted my head, and began inspecting my arm.

"What the hell happened?" She asked.

Mom shook her head. "Nothing. She's fine."

"No, she's not. We're leaving to the hospital right now." She gently held my left hand and we proceeded to leave.

Mom argued about it on the way out, but finally gave into Grammie's demands.

When we arrived at the hospital, we were escorted to a room to have my wrist looked at. Grammie sat next to me and petted my hair. The doctor came in and examined my wrist which he said was broken. We were informed that I needed a shot before placing my cast.

I froze.

I don't want to do that.

He left the room and I clung to Grammie's arm, counting the minutes before he'd come back in again. When he did show up, the needle he carried with him was gigantic. I leaned my head down, closed my eyes and hoped for it to disappear when I opened them again.

"Okay. It's going to be just a small poke," he said.

I opened my eyes and stared at a closer image of the needle. "No. No. NO. It's going to hurt."

Grammie petted my hair again. "You'll be fine. After this is over, we'll go get you some new earrings at Five Points Mall, okay?"

I nodded. Grammie always had a way of making me feel comforted. She gave the doctor an affirmative look for him to go ahead with the shot. I closed my eyes tight and cried as the needle went in. Once that was over, the doctor worked on my arm and placed a cast on me. Grammie continued to sit with me the whole time and told me I was brave and reminded me that she loved me so much. I just wanted to stay with her and not think about anything else, but I knew Dad would be picking us up after his shift. That made my stomach queasy with worry.

What's he going to do when he sees the cast on my arm? He's going to be mad at me.

Dad came to Grammie's house around midnight to pick us up. I walked out of the kitchen into the living room and looked at him. He sat on the organ bench, waiting for us to come home with him. He stared at me and didn't say a word. I put my head down, afraid he'd hurt me again. After the incident, I tried to hide the cast behind my back whenever I went out, hoping no one would notice. I was embarrassed by it, but it was too big to ignore. The cast was on my right arm making it so I was unable to write at school. The teachers took notice, and they began to investigate. My parents told the authorities that I fell out of the apricot tree I had climbed, and people believed them because they knew I liked to climb trees. I wondered often what I did wrong and how I could make it all better. My parents put up a unified front and I said nothing. I didn't want to be beaten again when I got home.

There were moments that brought me joy. They were rare, but still present from time to time. Mom, Dad, and I would go to the Drive-in movies on the weekends. We'd take Dad's truck. It was just us enjoying each other for a while and I embraced those moments of closeness when I could. Dad and Uncle Steve built me my very first bike out of baby blue spare bicycle parts, equipped with a white banana seat. They would go dumpster diving behind a bike shop to see what parts were thrown away and they'd build a bike with it. I felt loved, supported, and free every time I'd get on the bike that Dad created special just for me. A favorite game I loved to play was *Hot and Cold*. We'd hide a ball of aluminum foil somewhere in the house and try to find it. Instead of calling it aluminum foil, I liked to say, "Let's hide the tuna foil." I have no idea where that came from or why I called it that, just that overtime it stuck.

Dad made silly impersonations of characters—Donald Duck was a common one he'd do.

He acted like Goofy, and he'd put his hat brim to the side just to be different. His way of connecting to people was by being funny. He made me laugh. I'd forget for a while that there was chaos or problems in our family and home.

Mom loved going to church every weekend. She dressed us up like little dolls and busied herself with makeup and did her eyelashes. I longed for her to spend time with me and show me how to do makeup, but instead I was her subject as she fabricated every detail, so everything appeared just right.

"Just perfect," she'd say.

We couldn't be late, or she'd explode with anger. It was important that we were on time and made a good appearance. Mom particularly enjoyed the relief society. She liked to make crafts, and she was good at it. She also enjoyed meeting people.

I was confused.

Why does mom seem so lazy in every other facet of her life, but perk up for relief society?

There began to be strange men with mom when she picked me up from school, that I started recognizing from the Sunday church meetings. Some of the men, I didn't recognize at all. They come over when Dad was at work. She danced and sang to them, including songs she personally wrote. There were times she'd pull a kitchen chair into the living room.

"I'm a great singer," she'd say, while she pranced around them, behaving in an odd manner.

I overheard some of the men asking Mom about Dad's clothes, that hung from the bedroom door hanger. She told them they were her estranged husband's who she was currently separated from.

Why is she lying to them?

I'm instructed to find a friend's house to play at because she had "things to do." My baby brother Trent doesn't seem to be a problem and she'd leave him in the crib.

I was the problem.

Often, Mom couldn't find a house to send me to and she'd peer around our tiny home, trying to figure out what to do with me. Her eyes landed on the small living room closet. She opened the door and ushered me in. I hesitated, protesting, as I eyed the darkness inside. Mom paused for a second and then went to the kitchen. She returned with a four-pack of wine coolers and handed it to me.

Why is she giving this to me?

I'm told I can't leave the closet until I have finished ALL four. That became a new commonplace for me to hang out.

She's my Mom. I did what she told me to. I was afraid of her wrath.

I was in the dark.

The closet smelled musty. I noticed the light bulb is on a string, and I reached for it, but I wasn't tall enough.

I sunk to the cement floor beside the broom and vacuum cleaner. My imagination and thoughts took over.

How far back does this closet go?

What else is in here with me?

I glanced around, on guard for spiders. I knew there were spiders in there. It was tight, and there wasn't even room to sit cross-legged. I pulled my knees up to my chest and clutched them tightly. I stared at the wine coolers and grabbed one from the pack.

I hesitated.

She said I have to drink them.

I twisted the top off and drank the wine coolers. At first sip, they were sweet like fruit punch. The more I drank, the more it became too sweet, and I grew sick.

My head felt fuzzy.

I found a pair of scissors in the closet and started cutting my hair.

I was a drunk six-year-old working in the dark.

One day when I returned after being sent off to a friend's house, I walked into the house, and the bedroom door was open. I went to find Mom, and she was in bed with a man I didn't recognize.

He's not my father.

They both were naked. The man got up, and I saw his penis. It's the first time I'd ever seen a grown man naked and it was shocking. Mom casually rolled over and started talking to me as if nothing was wrong. I glanced away, turned around, and went outside to climb the trees.

The number of men increased. I began seeing some that mom babysat for, and more men from church. I dreaded being sent to the closet, so I tried to find a place to go when Mom was preoccupied. Eventually, I had to come home. Mom threatened me with violence if I ever said anything to Dad and she continued to warn me that *she'll break my face* if I disobeyed her wishes. I knew she meant it. I kept quiet.

Sometimes when Mom would take a nap on the weekends, Dad would draw with me and make silly faces with big ears and a giant nose. In the quite moments, I wanted to tell Dad about the men that would come over to the house while he was away at work. It felt wrong, but I always paused because I knew when he got mad at Mom that somehow it would always come back to hurting me.

A few months later, I came home from school and walked down the dirt driveway just like I did every day.

Dad was still home.

What is he doing here? He should be at work.

My parents were outside the house having a heated conversation. Mom zigzagged, walking away from Dad.

Dad beelined right behind her like he was demanding an answer to something she said.

He seemed insistent on Mom responding.

My shoulders tightened and I clenched my jaw.

Here we go. What's going to happen to me? Another broken arm?

I slowly walked a few steps and paused, trying to see if I could hear what they were fighting about. I couldn't hear much, but I was surprised they were having this moment outside where people could see their less than perfect appearance.

What's happening?

I slowly began to move again.

Mom appeared to be avoiding Dad and continued to walk away, but he stalked after her yelling, and he persistently asked her questions. They both glanced in my general direction. I stopped, hoping maybe that couldn't see me, and in that moment, I had wished to be up in the trees instead of on the ground. They saw me and Mom reacted by charging into the house.

Dad followed her and I quietly stepped inside after them.

What's happening?

I'd never seen them like this before. Something was different and Dad never got angry with Mom in this way. When I came into the house, Dad braced mom's arms and held her down on my bed in the kitchen, continuing to demand answers. I clung to my stomach and sucked in a breath like the wind got knocked out of me. I began to understand what was going on when Dad mentioned finding another man's watch in their bed. Mom wouldn't respond to him. She turned to me and screamed for me to call Grammie.

My hands shook and my knees wobbled.

Stop it.

I ran to the telephone hanging on the kitchen wall, but I didn't remember Grammie's number by heart.

What do I do?

I stared back and forth between both parents, feeling helpless. I didn't want them to hurt each other.

"I don't know the number," I said.

Dad started walking toward me and I braced myself for impact.

I'm in trouble now.

I flinched as he got closer. Dad took the phone from me and called his mom, Grandma Salter. I let out a breath I didn't even know I was holding, relieved to not have the phone anymore. I retreated to the living room and held my hands.

Are mom and dad not going to be together? What's happening?

I pouted. Dad continued his brief conversation with Grandma Salter and hung up the phone.

When Grandma Salter and Bill, my step-grandfather, arrived, Dad's anger subsided as they gathered around the kitchen table.

Mom stared at him. "I'm leaving, and I want to be with someone else. I'm taking Trent."

What about me? Am I of no importance to her?

Dad knelt in front of mom, holding her hands as she sat at the kitchen table. He cried, begging Mom to stay, and told her he didn't want to lose her even after what she did. "I'll forgive you. We can start over," he said.

My mind swirls with so many questions about how Dad would be able to take care of me with a 3:00pm-12:00am shift. That's when I'd be out of school.

Where will I go while he's at work? Will I be alone?

I gazed down at the couch. The abuse would no longer continue if Mom wasn't there, and I felt happy about that.

What will life be like now?

I held my hands together as mom went and packed her things, grabbed Trent, and left.

What's next?

Their marriage was over.

the calm before the storm

WHEN MOM AND DAD split up, it led to an oddly peaceful period. Kind of like the calm before the storm.

Mom moved away from our Layton home to live in Salt Lake City with the man she'd been caught with. His name was the same as Dad's—Roger. That was weird. I knew him as the naked man I found in bed with mom just a few weeks earlier. Off she went, leaving a trail of wreckage in her wake. She took my baby brother Trent with her but left me behind, throwing me away. Being a parent never seemed to be her priority.

Something had changed inside Dad, and he never hit me again. It was like Mom had cast some dark spell over Dad, something that brought to life the *darkest* parts of his soul—and now the spell had lifted. Dad was a single parent who worked crazy hours. I still had four months left of school. Dad was around to see me off in the morning but wouldn't be back until late at night.

There was no one to look after me when I got out of school. I was in second grade.

Dad had arranged with the church bishop for me to live with him and his family during the week, and on the weekends, I'd spend time with Dad. I didn't know the Woodbury's very well other than from church and that they lived in the same neighborhood, only two streets over.

Dad and I went to officially get more acquainted with the Woodbury's before I became their weekday live in. Dad knocked on their door, and it quickly opened. We were greeted by two smiling faces and an open greeting to come in.

"Tiffany, you remember the Woodbury's?" Dad asked.

I nodded.

Mrs. Woodbury put out her hand. "It's nice to see you. Let me show you around our home."

I hesitated for a moment before I took her hand. "Okay."

She proceeded to walk me around their house, showing every room, and not missing a beat. When we entered the theatre room, I paused and peered at the space in front of me.

Wow, this is going to be amazing.

After the house introduction, Dad took me to school on Mondays and I'd stay with the Woodbury's the rest of the week. There was food on the table every night and I got to do what "normal" kids did. I played at the park, listened to music, watched movies, and I didn't feel afraid to come home. The Woodbury's lived in a big house. It seemed giant to me, and they had French doors which appeared quite fancy and luxurious. A park was directly across the street from their home, where I played marathon sessions of hide-and-seek, sardines, and kick the can with the Woodbury children and the other kids in the neighborhood. When the streetlights came on, that was our cue to come into the house for the evening.

The Woodbury's had a piano that I liked to bang on, and I slowly began to learn how to play. I loved their huge basement where they had the home theater system with a drop-down projector screen. We watched a lot of movies and had many sleepovers with kids from the neighborhood. The surround sound was great for listening to music, too. I heard Dave Matthews Band and Doris Day for the first time while staying with the Woodbury's. The oldest daughter, Stephanie, went to High School but I liked the music she enjoyed. The Dave Matthews Band song "Satellite" played, and I instantly fell in love.

Once a week, they'd have breakfast for dinner, and serve pancakes, eggs, bacon, and toast. It was the first time I ever had "dinner breakfast." I thought the Woodbury's had taken out the patent for being cool parents after that.

Mom was nowhere to be seen. She never came to visit me, just vanished and left me behind. I often wondered if she was okay and when she'd come back.

Does she even care about me at all?

Will I ever see her again?

If she doesn't come back, I won't have to deal with the chaos.

When will she be back?

Never mind. I don't care if she's gone.

My mind was a war zone, never quite knowing which side to take as my heart wanted love and family, but I shielded to protect myself so I could survive.

No one hit me or locked me in the closet at the Woodbury's, yet, I felt out of place.

On the outside, life was good.

Except that it wasn't.

When Mrs. Woodbury would tuck me in at night, it felt weird and foreign. She would hug me and give me a kiss on the forehead just as she did with her own children, but we hadn't built that relationship. I didn't really know her. It felt like I was the consolation prize to Mrs. Woodbury and that she was obligated to do the same things for me that she did for her family. I didn't have emotional connections with the Woodbury's. Maybe it was the lack of love and affection I received from my parents, or perhaps it was because the abuse I had experienced had already taken a toll on my self-esteem, and I couldn't accept letting anyone in. I wished it was mom tucking me in at night. I had never had that from her.

The feeling of not belonging consistently sat deep down in my heart. The embarrassment of my parents being divorced was bad enough all by itself, but losing my home and parents, I felt very exposed. The Woodbury's would lend me clothes to wear to school because Dad couldn't afford new clothes for me. Most days, I'd wear the SAME clothes by choice. I especially loved the pink long-sleeved top and pink polyester bottoms that I often wore.

They were my favorite!

I felt special and confident in this outfit. "Accidents" occurred often where I would wet my pants. Mrs. Woodbury tried to convince me to find something different to wear for the next day while my *special* clothes got washed.

"No. I need to wear this outfit." I cried.

I didn't budge.

She smiled and left the conversation alone, putting the outfit into the washer. It was a very loved and washed outfit. Kids made fun of me for wearing the same thing every day, and Dad got called into school to talk with my teacher about it. I cringed when Dad came to discuss my family situation with my second-grade teacher. After the conversation, I felt like everyone was staring at me and I just wanted to curl up in a ball and disappear.

It didn't help that Mom got kicked out of the church for being with multiple men, *and I was living with the local church bishop.* No one ever said anything to me. Everyone was always pleasant, but emotionally the stirring within me said that people silently looked down on me.

On the weekends, I saw that Dad was struggling, but he stayed silent about it. I never saw him pray, and he didn't talk about faith or what church meant to him.

Why do we go to church?

Is it because I live with the bishop?

Is this what Dad wants?

I went through the motions of what I thought was the right thing to do based on my surroundings and how the Woodbury's lived their life. Dad and I had a few interviews with the bishop for me to get baptized into the LDS Church. Where I grew up, being baptized was a big deal. Every kid seemed to do it. Dad took the necessary steps to be able to perform this ordinance himself. It seemed important to him because it was important to me.

On the day of the baptism, I met Dad in the water. I was nervous about getting dunked because I hated water getting into my nose, but I was proud to have my dad there with me. His hands shook as he placed them on my head. He forgot what to say and had to start the prayer over a few times.

Shortly after I was baptized, we didn't go to church anymore and Dad began smoking.

What changed?

Did he not believe anymore?

It didn't really phase me as I was going along with what I thought I should've done.

The best part of the week was when I would stay with Dad on the weekends. I was no longer scared of him. Dad focused more on me, and we spent time together watching cartoons, catching a ball, or shooting hoops at the park, playing board games, drawing, or doing puzzles. He was really good at baseball and could hit home runs like no one's business. We often went to Kentucky Fried Chicken and got a bucket to go that we'd bring with us to the park. It was a treat for me. We went on bike rides together, and when he'd go out to work on his truck, I watched him.

It was peaceful.

I never felt at risk of being abused once Mom left. I had my Dad back. He was humble and content in his surroundings and never yearned for a life of luxury. He didn't talk about the lack of anything or the want of anything. The only time I saw him ambitiously excited was when he shared house development plans, back when he was with mom. That part of him was no longer present. Music was a big thing, and records lined the walls in his small house. Animated movies were also a favorite. Other than that, he was a simple man who'd go to work and come home. No extra responsibilities.

As school ended, the arrangement with the Woodbury's came to end. I couldn't stay with the bishop forever.

Where would I go now?

Summer arrived and things changed.

I disliked change.

empty promises

MY WORST NIGHTMARE HAPPENED. After four months of Mom leaving and saying nothing, she decided to reappear like a magic trick gone wrong. She showed up at the park across from the Woodbury House, and slowly walked toward me as tears streamed down her cheeks.

I stopped the swing I was on and glared at her. I pulled my headphones off and they clung around my neck as I held Dad's Walkman in my shaking hands.

Mom had reached out to me. "I just love you. You need to come be with me."

Who is this person?

I shook my head. I didn't move.

Dad will be alone. I'm not leaving.

"You're not going to change." I gazed up at her. "Things are just going to be the same."

She took a few steps closer to me. "Baby, I talked to your Dad. The court's agreed that this is the best option."

What? That can't be right? Why?

"Baby, I promise. Roger and I have a lot of plans on what we're going to change." Mom leaned down. "You're going to get a new room, and nice toys. It will be so much better this time."

No, it won't.

Mom stood up and began walking to the car. I stared at the ground, put my headphones back on, and followed a few steps behind her. I moved in with Mom and Roger in their apartment in Salt Lake City. I still saw Dad on the weekends, but Mom had full custody. On the weekends, mom drove us to Dad's work because his license got revoked from a hit and run, in grandpa's truck. We waited outside until work ended.

"Why do you need to go to the bank, mom?" I'd ask.

"Cause, I need to get *my* money," she'd say.

Your money?

She'd drive us directly to the bank to get the child support from Dad. I'd ask Dad if I could go inside the bank with him to get the money Mom needed for the weekend, and he always replied saying "Yes." It was a cool experience where I felt big and responsible doing this task with Dad, instead of feeling small like I typically did. It was a treat to me! Getting a sucker was an extra bonus, as well. Dad would pass the white envelope to mom like it was a secret letter, except only one person got something from it.

"See ya." Mom was disenchanting and cold as she would take her money. She didn't even look back before getting in her car and leaving.

I bunched my fist and clenched my jaw as I watched her go. Dad lugged Trent and I across Redwood Road in high traffic to get to the nearest bus stop. That made me nervous. I didn't understand why mom couldn't have dropped us off before she left.

Is this the reason why mom kept me around? For the money?
Why is mom getting the money now when Dad has us?
Where's the money going?

I disliked when the weekends were over because that meant we'd have to go back with mom. The moment I'd get into the house, Mom would be at the door, waiting with anticipation.

"What did you guys do?" She'd ask.

I smiled. "We went to the movies and got tacos. I also got a new outfit."

Mom placed her hands on her hips. "That's it? I *need* to know every detail."

I lowered my head. I went from a happy high spending time with Dad, to feeling rage and sorrow stepping back into a toxic house of abuse. "We hung out."

"That's not good enough," she yelled. "Where did you go first? How much did he spend on you?"

There she was stealing my joy. I sneered at her. "Is that a new dress?"

She paused and posed for me just like she did with some of the guys that came to our house. "You like it?"

I nodded and walked past her. The last thing in the world I wanted to do was live with Mom. I wasn't scared of her, but I was mad at her for ripping our family apart. She was the one who stayed with other men and had left us without any attempt to make things work. I blamed HER. Yet, there we were, mother and daughter, living together once again. At first, things were good in Salt Lake City. I was happy to be living with my little brother Trent again. I'd really missed him. The *Woodwind Apartments,* where Roger and Mom lived, were a step up from our cramped little house in Layton. We lived on the second level of the three-story building. Our apartment had two bedrooms. The furniture was all new which was a change of pace from the hand-me downs and thrift shop specials that we'd bought to furnish the house in Layton. The apartment even had a fireplace that seemed luxurious and fairytale-like. I got to sleep in a *real* bedroom, even though I had to share it with Trent. We had bunk beds. I hated having to share my bedroom, but it certainly was better than having to sleep on a small twin bed in the kitchen at Dad's house every night.

Now that I lived in Salt Lake, Roger had become the new figure in my life. He appeared more financially sound than Dad and more able to afford nice things. I was happy, and a bit dazzled to have all these new possessions. Even though he and Dad shared the same first name, he was totally different than my quiet, mild-mannered, and socially awkward Dad. Roger was a former military police officer with close-cropped hair. He wore straight-legged jeans and steel tipped combat boots or high tops on the weekends. He drove a big red macho truck with roll bars and lights.

Roger was very nice to me when I first came to live with him. Nicer than Mom had ever been to me. Roger led the charge, and we did fun things together as a "family." We'd play mini golf, go out to dinner, shop for new clothes, and we even went to the movies on the weekends when Dad didn't have us. I loved going roller-skating at the 49th Street Galleria in Salt Lake on Friday nights. I was incredibly impressed at Roger's ability to roller-skate backward. Who knew that human beings were capable of such wondrous feats? I knew right away that I wanted to learn how to do that, too. I fell in love with it.

Roger seemed to love peppering me with gifts.

He bought me my very own bubble-gum machine, just like the one I had seen on the ABC After School Special. I felt pretty cool when I turned the silver handle, and a little double bubble gumball would come out. Roger nicknamed me "Bubble Gum Monster." When he'd call me that, I'd giggle.

One day, I came back from visiting Dad on our weekend, and there was a new waterbed waiting for me in my room.

A waterbed!

I couldn't imagine anything cooler than that. It even beat out the bubble gum machine. I let myself hope and believe that

Roger cared for me. I began to think that my luck was changing, and things were starting to go my way.

Maybe everything would work out okay.

Mom was still Mom—dramatic, temperamental, and self-absorbed. Roger would be out of the house all day at work, which meant, just like when Dad was away, Mom would spend all her time watching TV and eating junk food. Every day, I came home from school, and there would be Scott Baio on the TV in the living room, and Mom feasting on her goodies. Mom never offered any to me. She *barely* even acknowledged my presence.

Now that I was eight, a bit older from when we were living together with Dad, Mom saw me as her slave and servant.

"Go get my snacks and turn on the TV," she'd yell. "Go get Trent."

She routinely ordered me to take care of Trent for her while she lounged around. I was in charge of changing diapers, bathing him, folding his clothes, keeping him entertained, and watching after him to make sure he didn't cry or get into anything. She'd also demanded me to make lunch for Trent and myself while she sat on the couch watching her beloved soaps. Nothing was to disrupt her soap operas, especially General Hospital. That was still her favorite of all of them! That's where she got my name, remember?

If I disobeyed her in some way, there was hell to pay. She'd turn on me in a moment. The slightest offense, either real or *imagined,* was treated with outbursts of physical abuse. I never knew what would set her off, but once triggered, I knew what was coming. Mom would storm over my way, grab onto the sides of my face as hard as she could while screaming so much that she'd spit on me. Her death grip would leave bruises on my cheeks.

"Stop. That hurts," I'd cry.

Mom didn't stop and she would chase me into a corner and beat me with a belt; then she'd pull me up by my hair, yelling at me to get up and stop crying.

"You have no reason to cry," she'd say.

Sometimes she'd grab me so hard that she'd be holding clumps of my hair in her hand when she was done.

The physical abuse was only one part of the trouble brewing. The other aspect was the whirlwind of drama and psychological turmoil that she was determined to stir up. I began seeing how Mom could never resist pitting one person against another.

Does she enjoy the fighting or is there something wrong with her?

Is that why Dad would hurt me? Was she trying to put him against me?

Mom told Dad things about Roger, some true, some not. She had the ability to wind up Dad like a child's toy. He became defensive and reactive which would escalate into him going after Roger. I hated contention and would hide the moment I felt it coming. Their fights were a mess and frightening. Roger had been in the military and wasn't one to back down, and Dad had a fierce passion for Mom that backed his stance to protect her.

They'd fight a lot, and Dad went to jail a few times for attacking Roger.

Mom just sat back enjoying the live soap opera that she stirred up with her sinister ways.

Roger was a different story.

Something in him had changed from being playful and attentive, to being cold and dark.

Mom didn't have the power over him as she did over Dad.

Roger had terrible posture and hunched over often. He was tall, about six foot two, and he looked like a scarier, more stoic version of Barney Fife from the Andy Griffith Show, but he wasn't funny in the least. Roger's demeanor and soul-draining stare gave me the Heebie- jeebies.

He very rarely smiled.

Mom insisted that I called Roger "Dad." I felt like I was betraying my love for my REAL Dad by doing that. I refused. Mom kept at it, saying that Roger was Dad, also. Over time, I started to call Roger "Dad" just to stop Mom from bugging me about it. Living with Mom was a constant exercise in finding ways to not set her off—to keep the abuse away. I learned to pick my battles wisely with her, but I never won, no matter how long I held out. That was how Roger became "Dad." I grew angry with Roger for being the person who took Dad's place in our daily lives. His stained teeth from the cigarettes he constantly smoked and the bad breath he had from drinking coffee, disgusted me. There was something about Roger that left me feeling uneasy. His face was like stone. He'd peer at me with a scary and stern demeanor. There was an articulated coldness as he observed me like I was a piece of meat that he was making plans for later. Deep in his eyes, something dark lurked there.

Why is he staring at me in that way?

As I'd walk past him, I held my shoulders like I had an invisible shield that no one could get through.

His form of punishment was more psychological and twisted in nature. It was like a switch would flip inside him, and when it did, there was an evil streak that came out of Roger.

He didn't seem to care at all what pain his punishments inflicted on those around him. He'd press buttons, and give the silent treatment, sticking to it for days on end. It drove mom absolutely crazy. She hated being ignored. Attention was like oxygen to her, and so she would scream, beg, and cry for Roger to speak to her.

Roger never buckled under pressure.

No matter how much she plead with him, he wouldn't break. Once he had made up his mind, it was done—no matter what the consequences. Roger would hand out what felt like extreme punishments to me. I was grounded for a month for saying a dirty word that I had overheard some kids repeating at school.

A *whole* month.

That was the equivalent of being grounded for eternity for a kid, and during the summer months, it was torture—a "Roger

Special" form of torture. I could hear my friends playing outside, while I was a prisoner in my bedroom.

One Saturday, we drove back from running errands and shopping when Roger and Mom got into an argument in the car. Roger's "flip" switched, and he suddenly pulled the car to a stop.

"Get out of the car," he yelled.

Mom stared at him. It seemed like she wanted to say something, but didn't.

I sat quietly in the back, holding Trent's hand.

Is he trying to be funny?

His face was red like a tomato, and he peered at Mom with wide eyes. He didn't look like he was joking, but he couldn't be serious. Where would we go?

"Get out. NOW!" He slammed the steering wheel.

Mom opened the door and got out, then proceeded to get Trent out of the car. I followed behind him, holding my hands together.

"Wait. Please. I'm sorry," Mom said. "Don't go, baby. Let's talk about it, huh?"

He shut the passenger side door and drove off into the distance. Roger left us alone, clear across town, standing by the side of the road. My stomach hurt. Mom sat on the side of the road and cried. I pouted, waiting for him to come back to get us.

Come back. Why did you leave?

He didn't come back. Roger was gone. Mom calmed down long enough to call our neighbors to come and pick us up so we could get back home.

Eventually, he would come back. Mom and Roger would get into this cycle where they would fight. Roger would kick us out, they would figure it out, make amends, we'd move back in, and then they'd do it all over again.

Is this what marriage is like?

Why would you get married living like this?

Was arguing fun for adults?

Dad dropped us off one evening from spending the weekend with him. When I got into the house, Mom and Roger were fighting and I could feel that the switch in Roger had already been activated. Trent and I were home for only a brief moment before things escalated, and we were kicked out of the apartment with Mom.

Here we go again.

Not in the dark.

I didn't like the dark, and Mom, Trent, and I were thrown out into it, on the snow-covered street. Mom was pregnant with my baby sister, Trina. The temperature must have been near freezing and Trent had tubes in his ears.

The cold is going to hurt him.

I cupped my hands over his ears, trying to keep them warm. We huddled together standing in front of our building, shivering while Roger stayed nice and warm inside.

"What are we going to do?" I asked Mom. "Where are we going to sleep?" She didn't say anything, just stood there and cried.

Why isn't mom marching us back inside the apartment? Is she scared of Roger? Is she confused?

Tears streamed down my face as my body shook from the cold. I glanced up and squinted my eyes.

Is that Dad's truck? How could Dad be here?

My heart leaped with hope as the figure walked toward us, carrying a bag.

It *was* Dad.

He returned with Trent's ear medicine that he left in his truck when he dropped us off. He knew Trent couldn't go without it. I was so grateful that he had forgotten and had come right at this moment to help us.

"Dad!" I threw my hands around his waist, and he patted my back.

"What's going on here?" He directed the comment toward Mom. She gazed at him. "Roger threw us out, again."

Dad bunched his fists. "Go get in the truck and warm up. I'll be right back." He gave the keys to Mom and headed toward our apartment.

I reached out my hand to try and stop him, but he'd gone farther than I could reach.

The warmth in the truck helped my shaking body and Trent stopped crying. Mom peered out the window like she was looking at a ghost, keeping her eyes on a specific area of the apartment building, waiting. I had no idea how much time had passed, but I was grateful to be in a safe space. The truck smelled like Dad, and I liked that. Eventually, we were let back into our apartment.

Dad gave us a hug goodbye and we went back inside with Roger. I realized that night that "home" was not a place that I could ever count on for love and security. Fear sat on my chest thinking about when we would be "kicked" out again, or when we'd have to pack up our things and bounce around once more.

bouncing

SCHOOL DIDN'T OFFER MUCH relief from the drama on the home front. In third grade, I attended Woodrow Wilson Elementary. I hated it. We lived right off State Street, which was one of the main drags in Salt Lake City. To get to school, I had to walk past car dealerships and heavily trafficked streets. It was also one of the major drug dealing areas in town, where needles, trash, and baggies littered the ground. Mom and Roger made me walk to school alone. I was scared and felt fear that I'd get kidnapped, or someone would jump me. The unknowns in the surrounding area made that daily morning walk a harrowing experience.

Once I got to school, things were no better. It was a big city school, and being the "new kid in school," kids picked on me and were mean. Unfortunately, I was quite often the "new kid" from being bounced around all the time. "Barnes" being my last name also didn't help.

"Barnyard Commando."

"You small like a barn."

"One whiff of Tiff, you'll jump off the cliff," they'd chant.

It was crowded and loud. There were quite a few Hispanic kids there, which meant there was a lot of Spanish speaking going on around me. I'd felt uncomfortable that I didn't know what was being said when they would talk with each other. Sometimes they'd laugh in my direction as they spoke – and I wondered if they were talking about me or making fun of me in some way.

Maybe they were.

Maybe they weren't.

I just felt that constant nagging and wondering, which added to my sense of feeling out of place there. I *dreaded* going to school every day.

I remember picture day distinctly. I'd gotten up early to get dressed and do my hair. I made the long walk to school down the busy streets and past the car dealerships. Just before I'd arrived at school, something wet landed on the back of my neck. I touched it to see what had landed on me, and white bird poop covered my fingers.

No! Not today.

When I got to school, I raced right to the bathroom and realized that I had bird poop in my hair and on the back of my shirt as well. I washed my neck and then put my hair in the sink to rinse it out. I grabbed some powder soap and lathered it into my hands, placing it into my hair to get the smell out. I rinsed again, turned off the faucet and stared at myself in the mirror.

I gasped and covered my mouth.

This is not happening.

The soap made my hair look even worse as white specks clumped throughout, making it look like bad dandruff.

"What are you doing?" My teacher asked as she held the bathroom door open. "Are you washing your hair in the sink?"

I turned to look at her, then at my soapy hands, and stared at her wide-eyed without saying a word.

"I'm calling your parents right *NOW.*"

She nodded toward the door, and I took the cue to follow her out. I held my head down as my wet hair dripped on the floor leading to the principal's office.

As if I didn't have enough things to be made fun of already. Pictures didn't happen that day for me, and I had to do retakes on a day when I wasn't needing to get bird poop out of my hair.

With no comfort at either home or school, I found myself searching for a place to escape to. Without any real-life hideaways available, I turned to the next best thing—*video games*!

Our apartments sat right behind the Ritz Classic Bowling alley. There, I discovered the joys of Mortal Kombat, Donkey Kong, and Teenage Ninja Mutant Turtles. Yes, I was a total tomboy. I found that boys were easier to be around and *far* less dramatic. Although, I did have some best girlfriends, as well. They were much like me because they also lived in abusive homes, in some way or another, and they were tomboys too. It was nice to feel understood.

All week, I saved up the money I found on my walks to and from school to go and play those games at the arcade in the bowling alley. I didn't have much money, so I learned that if I wanted my quarters to last, that I needed to get pretty good at the games so that I could play for hours on end just on those few quarters. I played against the boys in the neighborhood. They'd be so impressed when I would beat them in our video game showdowns. It felt good to actually impress someone. Those games were my escape. I stared at screens and played, not wanting them to end because it meant I had to go home—back to reality.

Another vehicle of escape was my beloved Huffy bike. If I didn't have any quarters for the video games, I would hop on my bike and just ride. One of my favorite things to do was to go up and down the street, stopping at each mailbox and pretend that they were make-believe places. One would be the grocery store, one the post office, another the zoo or aquarium. I would stop at each "location" and do a little skit, pretending I was far away. I wanted to be somewhere simpler, that was less hurtful than my school or home.

Of course, sometimes, reality would intrude on my little escapes. Once I was on my bike and wiped out in the apartment parking lot. I split my knee wide open. It was a really deep cut, and quite a bit of blood poured from it. I held my knee and limped inside, screaming in pain.

Mom and Roger both stared at me when I came in, but they didn't rush to my aid. They didn't say anything or ask if I was okay. They didn't take me to the hospital or to a doctor, in fact, they didn't seem too worried about at all. Mom wiped my knee up with a dish towel and placed a small band aid on the area, that covered only a small portion of the cut. I didn't care, I just wanted to get back on my Huffy and leave the house away from Mom and Roger. It would take more than just a gashed knee to keep me from getting back in the saddle.

My weekends with Dad were also an escape for me. I counted the minutes until he would come to pick Trent and I up. We went bowling, played basketball at the park, enjoyed picnics, swam, played Skee-ball or pinball, and went to the movies and got popcorn and drinks. My favorite thing to do with Dad was SHOPPING. Often, Dad gave Trent and I an "allowance" of about $10-$20 a weekend each to spend on what we wanted. It didn't matter to me what we did as I was just happy to be with him. I didn't care that he had used furniture or little money. It was nice to be somewhere where I felt safe and loved. Dad's yard invited me to play as sounds of crickets and birds greeted me, and in the summertime, sometimes we'd sleep outside on a mattress that we'd place under a big tree. Dad tried to be a good dad, but sometimes life with him was just as hard as with Mom.

One weekend, we went with Dad to get some snacks at the store. It was the summer of my 10th birthday and Trent's 4th. It was late. As we were walking back to his place, I could see a few police cars in the driveway.

I peered at Dad. "Why are there police at your house?" He didn't respond, but he had a look of concern on his face.

What's going on? Who's hurt? Is Dad in trouble?

I clung tighter to the grocery bag and my legs didn't want to move to find out what was happening, but Dad didn't slow down, and I needed to be with him. As we got closer, my heart thumped through my chest. The police informed him why they were there and that he was going to be taken in for having multiple outstanding warrants.

No! You can't leave us.

I wanted to run to him as my insides screamed to not let this happen. Trent wrapped his arms around my leg and cried. I placed my hand on his little back and I cried, too, begging them not to take Dad away as they handcuffed him and placed him in the car. I held Trent's hand and bent down to hug him, trying to keep his focus on me.

Dad. No, Dad.

A police officer called Uncle Scott to come and get us before they left with Dad. My begging didn't work to keep him with us, instead I saw him disappear around the corner, not sure when I'd ever see him again. He'd been in and out of jail for a year a now, but this was the first time I'd ever seen him taken away by police before. It felt more serious and uncertain.

We stayed that night at Uncle Scott, Dad's little brother's house. He also lived in Layton.

I didn't like that it was so late and that someone had to come get us at that hour of the night.

Shortly after, I began writing in my journal more as I tried to understand what I was feeling and what was going on around me. I chose to name my journal Aubree. It felt like a safe space to get things off my chest and express freely without fear of repercussions. The anxiety that I continued to experience about Dad's safety had heightened immensely. I worried about him getting hurt in jail by people who didn't care about his well-being. I feared that if he did get out of jail, when would be the next time the police would pick him up and he'd be taken back in.

Mom took us to see Dad a few times, and I felt grateful to her for doing that. My stomach tossed and turned, walking up to the jail with Mom. My mind told me that only people that hurt others stayed here. Criminals. Dad didn't deserve to be in this space that locked him up and caged him like an animal. I didn't see that in him. My shoulders tensed as I stared up at the guards that gave us clearance to see Dad when we went inside. I stayed close to Mom as we walked to where Dad was being held. It was loud in jail, and every sound seemed to echo back and forth off the walls, filling my ears with ringing and confusion.

Dad gazed at us with excitement, but quickly peered down at the ground before meeting my eyes again. He looked like himself, but the bold letters on his jumpsuit that said Davis County Jail, and the sorrow that I saw in his eyes, told me he wasn't the same. Things had changed for him and seeing him like that haunted me.

CHAPTER SIX

a revelation

WHEN DAD GOT OUT of jail, I was so relieved to see him and to see that he was okay. It was a mess at times being with him as I never knew when and if he'd be back in jail again, but when he was around, I always felt that he wanted me there with him. The worst part of every weekend was when Sunday would wind down, I knew it was time to go back to Salt Lake City. My stomach gurgled with unease, and it hurt from tightness that seemed to come from the nerves I was feeling from going back with Mom. I'd be in and out of the bathroom. I dreaded Sundays and the way they made me feel emotionally and physically sick.

Mom kept Dad wrapped around her finger, and Dad still loved Mom even though they were going through nasty divorce proceedings. Mom liked nothing more than to create drama and chaos, and she continued to hook up with Dad from time to time. I didn't want them to be together. Rage filled within me directed at both of them for behaving this way.

Why can't Mom leave Dad alone?

Why does Dad keep taking her back?

Why is Mom continuing to bounce us around?

Can't Dad see how amazing he is and that he deserves better?
Don't be with her.

I didn't know if some part of Mom still cared for Dad, or if she wanted to press Roger's buttons, or if it was all about creating controversy. All I knew was that it meant *trouble* for me.

Roger's relationship with Mom grew worse. A lot of the chaos appeared to be because Mom was still hooking up with other men and occasionally Dad.

"Who were you with last night?" he'd scream.

Before Mom could say anything, he'd throw the entire family out of the house. Not just for a day or a night, like he used to, but weeks and *months at a time.*

This became the "bouncing" period. Mom and Roger would fight, and as a result, we would leave. Pregnant Mom, Trent, and I would go live somewhere else for a while, Mom and Roger would reconcile, and we would return to Salt Lake City, again.

It didn't take long before they would fight again and off we went, bouncing once more. I lived with every variation of my family during that period. We'd go to Aunt Sherry's, on Dad's side, and Dad would stay there with us. Or, we'd go to my Aunt's on Mom's side, Aunt Dora.

Most often, Mom would retreat to her parents— to Grammie's house.

The various family members we lived with were scattered all over the Salt Lake Valley. It made no difference for Mom, who did not have a job and was pregnant, and Trent, who was still a toddler. But for me, it made a HUGE difference. When Mom would leave Roger, she'd just up and pluck me out of school, take me with her, and then dropped me in the new school wherever she landed. I was in and out of so many different elementary schools during this period, I couldn't even remember them all. I quickly learned to acclimate to the many different environments and living situations I found myself in. There were many, all driven by who mom was with and what kind of relationship they had at the time.

Kids at school didn't understand.

I didn't understand.

"How long are you here for this time?" They'd ask.

Great question, and one that I never knew the answer to, so I'd shrug and look down at the ground. I started giving up on making friends because I knew I'd be leaving again soon. I began conditioning myself not to get too close because I knew they would most likely be taken from my world at a moment's notice. Sometimes, I just wanted to break down and cry for hours, letting it all out. I wanted to run in any direction Mom wasn't.

Why can't you stay put, Mom?

Why can't you stay with one person and stop messing with our lives?

I wanted to yell at her. I wanted to express my true feelings about how angry and resentful I felt inside from her dragging me around like a rag doll with no regard to my feelings or what impact it may be having on my life. Instead, I kept it all tucked away and out of sight. It seemed easier that way. As a result, I became withdrawn. I had no real friends. I didn't try to do my schoolwork and retreated more inward. I became a sad and quiet girl, hurting so much on the inside, but kept up a face of complacency. It was easier to an extent to keep to myself, but lonelier. Packing from one place to another exhausted me physically and emotionally. Every time I tried to put down roots, it felt like I would be yanked up and placed somewhere else.

I didn't want to be living in someone else's house. It meant always adjusting to their ways of living and constantly feeling like a guest when making the rounds from place to place. Things had been bad back in Salt Lake City, but at least I knew what to expect every day. At least before there was some order, it was a painful order, and it wasn't fun walking down State Street to school, but at least I knew where I was going to school each day. This wasn't healthy for me.

Aunt Mallory came in from California and hadn't seen Mom for a long time. She seemed short and frustrated with Mom, but excited to see us.

"Why do you treat your kids like this?" she asked. "They need to stay in one place. You shouldn't be bouncing them around."

Mom threw her hands in the air. "How dare you tell me how to parent?" She dragged me out to the car shortly after that. The confrontation between them stayed with me because in that moment what my aunt said gave me validation and made a lot of sense. Before her, no one ever said those things out loud to Mom. It was the first time I felt looked out for. Like my aunt said, I *did* want to stay in one place, but I was a little girl and still under Mom's control. I went where she told me to go.

I was horrified that my mother seemed oblivious to the fact that her children were suffering. I resented her for putting my brother and me through that hell. But what chilled me to the bone was that she didn't see what she was doing. It didn't seem to faze her one bit.

Mom didn't appear to think twice about the consequences of her actions on her children. Her selfishness utterly blinded her.

A part of her seemed to love the drama of it all. She thrived on chaos. The spinning from the twister she liked to create was her natural environment. At the same time, the storm tossed about her children without any warning of when it would hit. Mom, at times, became an overpowering bully. She'd blow the doors off anyone who tried to get into her business. When she turned on you, it was like a hurricane blowing—FULL FORCE. I felt for anyone that might try to get in her way. Even her mother, a kind and decent woman was not exempt from these storm blasts from Mom.

Grammie was always a listening ear, a loving anchor, someone to lean on and talk to. She supported Mom in many ways even when she probably didn't deserve the help. Mom would come by Grammie's house, drop us off, and barely communicate or connect with Grammie.

They were not affectionate with each other. I could see the disappointment on Grammie's face as Mom would leave. She never said anything, but quickly changed her demeanor into a smile around us. I often wondered what happened for them to have this relationship, and why Mom was being so mean. Grammie had been very affectionate and nurturing with me. She was known by many, as the "Love you, Lady" because she loved everyone and she'd let them know, even people she just had met. Grammie expressed kindness and love wherever she'd go. People would call her often and vent. She'd sit on her stool by the phone in the kitchen and listen, sometimes for hours. She was an inspiration to me and many others.

It confused me.

Why are Mom and Grammie so emotionally distant like this?

When Mom would come back, she'd yell at Grammie about all the things she didn't do.

"Why didn't you finish up all the homework with Tiffany?"

"Why is Trent dirty? Did you forget to give him a bath?"

"We're you even watching the kids?"

"Why are you helping her with her bloody nose. She can figure it out on her own."

I found Grammie crying may times over the hateful and distasteful things that Mom would scream at her, the one person who was truly trying to help her. It was like Mom was scolding Grammie, as if *she* was a child.

Stop hurting Grammie.

I bunched my fists.

I will protect you.

My heart hurt seeing her like this and taking all the mean comments that were being handed to her. Grammie didn't fight back, and she didn't yell at Mom. In fact, she never yelled at anyone. I wanted to fight for Grammie and tell Mom how wrong she was for treating people this way. But, I felt small and lacked self-confidence. I often questioned myself. This was no exception, so I kept quiet.

Deep down in my soul, I knew the world of chaos that I lived in was not the only possibility. The episode with Aunt Mallory was the beginning of something inside me. A slow, expanding realization grew in me that I didn't have to live the way Mom did. This understanding started to take root during the time I spent living at Grammie's during our bouncing around. In all the moving, their home was the place where we landed the most.

Amidst all the chaos and confusion of the bouncing period, my time with my grandparents was a true blessing. It was the first moment in my life I was really in a loving and supportive family environment for an extended period. The time with my grandparents, not just visiting, but living with them, was a revelation. I began to learn there was a simpler and happier way to live beyond Mom's madness and that this was not just a dream or fantasy but a real thing.

I could be happy and deserved to be!

a soft place to land

MY GRANDPARENTS LIVED in a quiet, all-American suburban town called Woods Cross. It was a far cry from the bustling and scary world in Salt Lake City. Woods Cross predominantly appeared to be LDS, a Mormon religion, as much of Utah was. Everyone on the street took great care of their yards and homes. Their edging was clean, trees well-kept, the grass grew green and lush, and flowers thrived and bloomed. Nothing dead or dried out appeared down our street. Neighbors would bring over dinner or a plate of cookies for another neighbor when someone was sick, or they'd come by just to say hi. I enjoyed how polite and friendly everyone was. I liked that no matter where I went in the neighborhood, I always felt safe. It was a tribe and community where everyone seemed to know one another and looked out for each other. The elementary school was just the next street over from Grammie and Grandpa's house, so it was a quick walk to school. I really liked that. I would often go back to school after it was out to play on the playground or play games on the field. I loved the environment and reveled in the peace and calm I found myself in.

My best memories living with Grammie and Grandpa mostly revolved around food. Maybe it was because Grammie made the best meatloaf ever, or because a home-cooked meal was always waiting for me when I got home. Perhaps, it was because of my sweet memories of making cookies, pie, and dumplings with her. She was well known for her unique "Hush- Puppies," similar to a hot pocket. I loved them so much that I would always beg her to make them. Everything Grammie made was delicious and created with love and care. Her food was symbolic of the nurturing that was present in her house.

Whenever I would come home from school, she already had started the evening dinner preparations in the kitchen. She always greeted me with a big hug and a kiss asking me how my day at school was. Then she would say, "Go wash your hands and come help me with supper."

Grammie made EVERYTHING from scratch. I loved that about her. She would even make homemade cherry pop tarts for me in the toaster for breakfast before school. When we made hush puppies, she let me stand up on a stool and roll the dough out on the counter. Then when the meal was ready, she would shout, "Supper's ready!" I would go running to the table in excitement to see what wonderful meal awaited me. Food was not just about eating, but also a chance for us to hang out and have fun together. For an outwardly mild-mannered woman, Grammie had a silly secret streak inside her.

Sometimes we would eat "Malt-o-Meal" together for breakfast. Grammie would usually sit down and eat breakfast with me, and we pretended we were robots and move in sections while we ate. Seeing Grammie act like a robot would make me laugh so hard I could barely swallow my milk without it spilling out of my nose! We'd have so much fun, we'd lose track of time, and I would have to run to school so I wouldn't be late.

Grammie was also a borderline diabetic, so she wasn't supposed to eat much sugar. But sometimes, when we were watching an old movie together, she would send me out on a stealth mission to get us a secret sweet snack. I would tiptoe into the pantry and get us a cookie, ice cream or a piece of cake. It was fun sneaking around like we were spies on a secret mission.

Grammie was so much fun!

Besides cooking, Grammie loved her old black and white movies. At first, I resisted and wanted to watch The Mickey Mouse Club instead, but it didn't take long for me to fall under the old movie's spell. Grammie had a little library of movies that she had recorded off of the American Movie Classics Channel. Almost every day after school, we would watch the classics: Casablanca, The Apartment, It's A Wonderful Life, Gone with the Wind, anything with Humphrey Bogart or Audrey Hepburn—and her favorite The Wizard of Oz. Grammie loved to sing and was a beautiful whistler. She enjoyed the musicals and would sing right along to all the songs. We must have watched that one at least once a week!

My favorite, of course, was Breakfast at Tiffany's because it had my name in the title. Plus, I thought Audrey Hepburn was so pretty.

The movies appealed to me because they seemed to represent a simpler time. I would lay across Grammie's lap, and she would tickle my back with her long nails while I imagined what it would be like to live in that wonderful world with Audrey Hepburn. I think she felt the same way. Everyone always appeared to have beautiful skin and clothes, and fancy hats. Grammie would often sing me a song from "Guys and Dolls."

"I love you a bushel and a peck, a bushel and a peck, and a hug around the neck." It quickly became one of my favorites.

It was our thing.

Grammie and I also loved to play games together, especially card games. Rummy was my favorite. It was basically a sin if you're a girl in my family and do not know how to play rummy. I could always remember a rummy game being played somewhere in Grammie's house from my earliest years. After years of practice, I developed my skill and became really good at it. In time I finally was able to beat Grammie! Whenever I would win, she would chase me around, tickling me, saying, "I'm going to get you, Doll Face."

"You know why I call you Doll face?" She'd ask.

I shook my head and smiled at her.

Grammie smiled back at me gently holding the bottom of my chin. "You have such a beautiful face like a doll." She asked a very close friend of hers, Ida May, to make a doll that resembled me. I loved it so much. I named it Ida May after her. Grammie was more than just food, movies, and all the other sweet things she would do for me. She was the essence of home, filled with safety and love. It was wonderful to laugh, love deeply and enjoy the world with someone. Grammie was fun, unassuming, and down to earth, all of which was a breath of fresh air for me. I could be myself around her. I didn't have to worry that the slightest unintentional act on my end, setting her off somehow. Instead, she made me feel comfortable and special, two things I had very little experience with.

Every night she would tuck me into bed with a kiss and then gently tickle my back until I fell asleep. And what a bed it was. I didn't know how Grammie did it, but the sheets felt fresh and clean every day. She made the bed nice and tight so that when I got in, it was like my own personal cocoon. I felt safe and loved in that bed. So warm, cozy, and familiar.

I *finally* felt at home.

Grammie's house also had a sense of order to it. Things happened in a set fashion, and that was a revolutionary concept to me. Grandpa went shopping every Friday for groceries. There was a list kept on the fridge of what the house needed. He would get what was on the list, and I could add items that I wanted. I could put vanilla ice cream with chocolate syrup on the list, and on Friday it would be in the house.

It was like paradise. Grandpa enjoyed eating ice cream with me after dinner, and we'd make our ice cream delights together. It consisted of a perfect blend of chocolate syrup, vanilla ice cream, hard-shell chocolate covering, cherries, and occasionally cool whip.

Yum!

Every Friday, we had a bubble gum blowing contest at school where whoever blew the biggest bubble would receive a prize. Grandpa made sure that I had a new pack of Bubblicious gum each week, ready for the big day. I practiced by the fireplace, showing Grammie what I could do.

Pulling the gum off my eyebrows and nose, I declared to Grammie, "I think I'm going to win."

Grandpa encouraged his grandkids to learn an instrument. He was a talented musician who played the piano and the organ for the Jay Welch Choral.

One day Grandpa approached me with a big smile on his face and his hands behind his back. "Look what I have for you. You should try the violin." He brought his hands forward and gave me a violin.

My eyes grew wide. It looked so fancy and delicate.

Wow!! This is for me? I get to play this!

"Thank you, Grandpa." I took it from his hands and gave him a hug.

"You only have to practice on the days you eat," he'd say.

I paused and scrunched my nose. "That's every day." He smirked and nodded.

I practiced every single day just like he mentioned.

When I went to music class, the teacher suggested that I try the viola. There already were too many students with a violin, and she needed some violists. I reluctantly said OKAY. I had no idea what a viola was, until she showed me. It looked almost exactly like a violin. My teacher asked for my violin, and I handed it gently to her. She replaced the violin strings with viola strings and gave it back to me. When I got home from school that day, I rushed in the house to find Grandpa.

I hope he's not mad about the violin.

I turned the corner of the front room and nearly crashed into him.

"Where are you going so fast?" he asked.

I paused, then stared up at him. "My teacher changed my violin. They already have too many violin players and need violists. She changed the strings."

Grandpa's eyes grew wide, and he smiled. "That's okay. We'll get you an actual viola."

We went to Summerhays Music and traded the violin with the viola strings in for my very own viola that I got to pick out. He went into town and picked up new sheet music that he thought I'd enjoy, and on special occasions we'd visit the music store together. I also got into private music lessons. I felt fancy and pampered. My love for music was alive within myself and Grandpa and the viola began a life-long love of classical music.

It was one of the first times in my life that I had a healthy routine. It felt fun and loving and under control.

The biggest thing I had to worry about during this period was the local school bully—Ashley McNally. Every school had a bully or two. Usually, the trick was just avoiding them, but I somehow managed to land a target on my back when it came to Ashley. The funny thing about Ashley was that she looked remarkably similar to a bull. She was stocky and fierce-looking and seemed ready to charge at any moment. I used my wits to find a way to fight back. I would use her weight as my ally to get back at her. I teased her by saying, "Go ahead, and meet me after school! I'm not afraid of you. The only thing I'm scared of is your big butt bouncing me to the moon!"

My biggest advantage against Ashley was living just around the corner from the school.

On the days that Ashley threatened to beat me up after school, I would go out the school's side door. It was the closest exit to my grandparent's house. I stepped out and made a run for it, praying that Ashley and her entourage of bully friends wouldn't see. I had several close calls, but she never caught up to me. I pretended I wasn't afraid of her, but deep inside I said a prayer that I could somehow run away fast enough that she wouldn't catch me. The fact that the worst thing I had to worry about was the school bully was a great relief. I was afraid of the same scary things that other kids worried about and that felt like I'd been granted a reprieve from the unique world of chaos and abuse that I lived.

When Mom and Roger got back together for the umpteenth time, Mom was getting ready to bounce me once again, taking us from staying at Grammie and Grandpa's house back to Roger's. We had been living with Grammie for a month—the longest period that we had stayed anywhere. Most of the time, we'd bounce after a week or two. I felt like I was *finally* placing some roots for the first time. I loved being in Grammie's care and I enjoyed the nurturing environment we lived in. I didn't want to go back to a life of chaos and confusion, and I had gained courage to speak my truth. I told Mom I wanted to stay and live with Grammie and Grandpa.

She shook her head. "We're leaving."

"No. I want to finish fifth grade at the same school. I'm staying." I was surprised that I stood my ground with her, something I had never done before. I was sick of being bounced around.

Mom's eyes widened, and she tilted her head backward, staring at me. She opened her mouth and paused. "If Grandpa says it's okay, then you can stay."

My arms tingled and my stomach leaped as I felt shocked that Mom was even saying this.

Could this be a possibility?

I gazed at Grandpa with excitement. "Can I?????!"

"Yes," he said.

I jumped up and down, clapping my hands. The energy of joy that filled within me felt as if I had just won a new viola. I let out a breath, and my chest loosened. The tightness I had been feeling for a while, released.

Mom left with Trent to live with Roger, and I stayed behind with Grammie and Grandpa.

My grandparent's house became my home, a loving place that Mom never provided for me. I enjoyed the fruit of being in one school for the whole year. Because I knew I was staying in one place, I became more present and allowed myself to focus on schoolwork, made friends, and tried new things. It allowed me to relax and engage. I got good grades, and I played basketball. When given a chance, I did well at school. It seemed so stable and rational compared to my domestic life. I won the science fair by designing a giant rubber band that could hold up to seventy-five pounds! Grandpa was so proud of me. He took me to the store to buy a frame for my certificate and ribbon. I entered the school spelling bee and worked so hard on every single word. I could do them all perfectly.

On the day of the spelling bee, I did very well until I ran into the word "cautious." My hands shook, and my throat became dry as I went to spell the word with a *C* instead of a *T*.

I ground my teeth and held the tears in knowing I had just missed the word.

Why did you mess up?

I liked getting recognized in my school and get positive validation from adults. I fed on the accolades. I really enjoyed hearing praise for all my hard work as it was not something I was used to. Fifth grade was the best and most productive school year.

I realized that I could have a life of my own separate from Mom's if I had the strength to stand up for it. The seeds of my strength started to appear. Slowly, I began learning how to carve out my own life and become an independent person.

I soaked in all the moments of this time with my grandparents before I had to go back with Mom. In truth, part of the reason I wanted to stay with my grandparents was because I liked having ice cream every night, watching old movies, eating home-cooked meals, sleeping on fresh sheets, and feeling my grandparent's love for me daily. I also appreciated the value of being my own person without being judged or controlled.

Something inside me stirred.

puberty

FIFTH GRADE ENDED AND dread clung to my shoulders knowing that this was the end of living with Grammie. I knew the feeling of weight and heaviness well, and I had just forgotten the familiarity of it while I stayed with my grandparents. Now it was back like a re-occurring nightmare. I thought about many possibilities on how I could stay another year with Grammie, and I hoped that for some reason Mom wouldn't want me back. I hoped I could stay longer and let the dread cling to someone else, and not be mine. But, alas, Mom wanted me back, so I moved back in with her and Roger at the beginning of sixth grade.

I wasn't thrilled at the prospect of going back to the old toxic behaviors, drama, uncertainty, and instability. Mom and Roger were now living in what I would come to call *The Blue House*. It was a baby blue-colored home in a little town outside Salt Lake City called West Jordan. The house was nothing special, just a split-level home on the corner. It had an unfinished basement, and the lawn was overgrown, but it was far removed from the drug dealing that had scared me so much on State Street. The neighborhood was quiet and peaceful. I wasn't afraid to walk the streets alone, and that was a great relief to me.

Mom became pregnant again, and this time she was having a girl! I was SO excited to have a little sister. My friend Sara and I made a big banner saying "WELCOME HOME" out of perforated computer paper to showcase when Mom and my new little sister came home. I went and visited Mom in the hospital, and when Baby Trina came home, I had visions of this being the change that might make us a happy family.

Things did change in the home environment for a while. There were now rules that made sense and were consistent. I only got punished when I did something wrong, unlike the harsh punishments Roger handed out previously. If I missed curfew or got an F, I'd be grounded, but it wasn't for months at a time. I was rewarded $5.00 for every A, or we'd be able to go get a piece of candy at the neighborhood Reams. My candy of choice was the giant jawbreakers that felt like it would take a month to consume, one lick at a time. I just kept wrapping it up to save for the next day. Every once in a while, I'd even get a new pair of basketball shoes when I did good work.

Maybe things will change this time.

But, all was not well in The Blue House, and this consistency didn't last long. My high hopes quickly began to slip away. Mom was still Mom no matter where or WHOM she lived with, and stability wasn't a thing to count on with her. If there was a calm, she'd be out of control shortly after with beatings and torture. I tried to stay off Mom's radar whenever possible Adding to the tension was the haunted house that we lived in.

For REAL.

I swear.

My life was already haunted enough and the last thing I needed was this new addition creeping on me, too. Strange things kept happening in the house. We discovered a large black star-like symbol painted on the wall in the unfinished basement and the local gossip was that druggies and devil worshippers had lived in the house before us.

One night, Mom thought she heard baby Trina crying. She got up to investigate and claimed she saw a strange man leaning over the crib singing to Trina. She recognized his face as Roger's father who had hung himself years before Mom ever met Roger, but she'd seen pictures of him in old family albums. Mom ran screaming back to the bedroom. When Roger went to look, there was no one in the room with the crying baby. Of course, no one believed Mom. Everyone thought she was being overly dramatic *again* as she did have a reputation. But, enough strange things happened in that house that she began to seem less crazy to me as I experienced them as well.

Multiple friends would come over at different times for a sleepover, and they wouldn't make it through until morning. They woke up in the middle of the night and demanded that their parents come and pick them up. They said they saw shadows in the nightlights and heard strange sound, and they didn't want to stay any longer. My neighbor and good friend, Shantal, stayed over at our home one night and mentioned seeing the door open a little on its own. She called her mother, in tears.

There were times Mom, my siblings and I, would be downstairs and toilets would flush on their own upstairs. Sometimes, we'd come home, and all the cupboards were wide open when no one had been in the house. It became much harder to ignore and pretend like nothing was going on. One evening, I fell asleep on the couch in the living room. I had broken my nose playing basketball that day and had been watching TV to keep my mind off the pain and discomfort. I also didn't like my bedroom being in the basement, especially because Stephen Kings "IT" just came out. We had a drain downstairs that made me think the clown would come through it to take me away. I felt more comfortable upstairs. I woke up suddenly in the middle of the night and saw someone standing by the railing at the top of the stairs. It wasn't a member of my family or anyone I recognized.

"Help me," my mind screamed.

Did anything come out?

I tried to move my feet to stand and race to Mom, but I couldn't move, scream, or react at all. I was frozen, watching it all in motion and unable to do anything.

It was the first time I'd ever seen something supernatural.

I didn't want to draw attention to myself more than what I'd experienced with bouncing, the abuse, and now having a black eye and bruised nose.

Would people question how I really got the broken nose?

Adding this paranormal situation to the mix wasn't something I wanted anyone to know about, but word got around about me living in a haunted house. I was never really scared of whatever the paranormal wanted. In some ways, the ghosts in the house were the least of my troubles.

Mom's behavior towards me grew worse.

It seemed the older I got, the more she hated having me as a daughter. I think some part of her enjoyed being a mom when I was younger. Babies were like playthings to her. She could dress me up in outfits and make me do modeling poses for her. Not in a sweet motherly way, but in a way for her to get her kicks, to show me off for her own gain. I was her own living Barbie doll—a toy, not a child. And now I saw her doing the same thing with Trina. It appeared she enjoyed the special treatment of people letting her cut in lines, holding doors for her, and getting the attention and privileges that having young children provided her. More than anything in the world, Mom loved being the center of attention.

Now that I was growing up, even that one small spark of interest in being a Mom disappeared. She focused all her attention on baby Trina. I was a burden to her, something she often said as a reminder, so I'd never forget.

I was in sixth grade and eleven-years-old.

I was no longer cute, and I no longer got her any special attention.

I was just a kid that needed a mother.

I don't think she knew what to do with the new responsibilities of having an older child.

It was hard work now, which was Mom's least favorite thing. The results weren't pretty and the physical abuse continued again unabated. Mom was a tiny person, slight, skinny, and only a few inches over five feet tall. I was nearly her height and getting stronger. Yet, she still had the power to smack me around when her temper reared its ugly head. She shoved me into a corner and threatened me with a belt. At other times, she'd pull me down the stairs by my hair, holding clumps of my hair in her hand as she continued to scream at me.

Roger demanded that Mom kept a clean and neat house, filled with home-cooked meals, that were presentable when he got home from work. She had four meals that were her specialties, and we circulated between each one. The menu consisted of Shake-N-Bake Porkchops paired with Au Gratin Potatoes, Goulash, Spaghetti, or Lasagna. Mom followed the orders that he put into place. She seemed afraid of him but didn't say anything about it just stayed focused on her tasks he gave.

Is she afraid of him like I'm afraid of her?

Did following orders keep her off his radar?

I didn't understand this dynamic with Mom because she couldn't be bothered to keep her kids clean. She never reminded me to take a bath or brush my teeth, and Mom didn't do the laundry. I was put in charge of that. If I wanted clean clothes to wear to school, I needed to have it done.

My body was changing and growing, and kids at school were becoming much more aware of their own and others' bodies. Mine was a mess, literally. I had a Mickey Mouse watch that I had gotten on a trip to Disney Land. I loved it and refused to take it off, wearing it day and night. The watch was one of the nicest things I owned, and I cherished it.

Once, when I was over at a friend's house, I took it off and placed it on the counter. Bunching her nose, my friend stared at me. "Oh my gosh. What is that smell?"

My shoulders tightened and I shrugged, feeling insecure. After some investigative sniffing, I realized all the sweat and grime that had accrued on the watch made for the stench she smelled. A blended smell of sour milk and stinky feet lived on my wrist.

I was mortified.

Mom had great awareness of her hygiene but teaching her oldest daughter anything on this front was of no interest to her.

I needed to find a way to survive the trials of puberty.

unhinged

PUBERTY NEVER APPEARED TO be an easy time for any kid. In my case, I had found it particularly difficult. As puberty kicked in, I began shedding my tomboy lifestyle and became much more of a girly girl. I started to replace days in the yards creating mud pies, hanging out in the treehouse, and playing sports with dressing my Barbie Dolls, making up dances with my girlfriends, and playing "House." My best friend Sara had MTV at her house, and I envied her for it. We became mesmerized by the music videos they played, watching them for hours at a time, especially Janet Jackson's videos. We were obsessed with watching her dance. Sara and I spent hours putting on make-up, dressing up in all black, and working on memorizing the moves from "Rhythm Nation" so that we could dance just like her. We loved to paint our nails, crimp our hair, and do everything as Janet did.

As I began to develop physically as a young woman, it seemed to trigger something in Mom. Strangely, Mom behaved in a competitive nature with me. As a result, things went from borderline bearable to extremely weird. She liked to think of herself as the prettiest woman in the room and was so proud of her figure.

"Look at how gorgeous I am," she'd say. "I'm so attractive."

It wasn't said in a way of body positivity, but in a taste of arrogance for how much better she thought she was.

Mom obnoxiously would point out to friends and family that I was growing breasts. "Can you believe she has bigger breast than me? Really seems unfair since she's only twelve." She liked to announce when it was period day to whoever was around. While I drowned in shame and embarrassment, she would proceed at times to ask my friends if they had gotten theirs yet.

"You know, only real women get their periods and have boobs." She'd say tauntingly to my friends.

It didn't help with my self-esteem and general worth with my pre-adolescent friends.

I loved having my friends over to do the Janet Jackson dances and other popular hits on MTV with me, but it grew to be less fun as Mom engaged. We would be minding our business, playing or making up dances when she'd butt in with me and my friends. "Watch out. I'm going to show you how dance." Mom pushed into us, making room for herself. "You know, I know how to dance way better than Tiffany. Let me show you."

I ground my teeth, holding in the roar I felt lingering in my chest.

She's taking over my time with *my* friends.

Other times, Mom would get out her karaoke machine. She'd would turn it on and demand us all to watch her dance and sing. No one really wanted to, but Mom's insistence won over, and we gathered around her and the prized karaoke machine. She danced sexually, shaking her butt, or humping the air.

"I'm so good at this." Mom said.

Oh my God.

I covered my mouth and had the urge to stand up and leave but didn't.

I wasn't impressed. I was mortified.

The world seemed to move in slow motion, spotlighting her.

This is pathetic.

It was as if she wanted to make sure she was the coolest kid in the gang.

Why couldn't she leave me alone and be happy with just being a mother who let their kids play and do their own things?

Mom really believed that she'd be discovered to be the next Debbie Gibson or Paula Abdul. Mom wanted to be noticed so bad that she'd go up the street to get help from my friend's dad, who happened to have a little room where they recorded her songs in exchange for sexual favors. Later, Mom and I spent hours filling manila envelopes with cassette tapes to make her dream come true with her hit, "Why," and her special edition song, "I Like Horses. You like Chocolate."

One night, I had some friends down in the basement with me where my bedroom was. We were making waterbeds out of zip-lock bags for our Barbie dolls, and planning elaborate fake dates with Ken, when Mom came flouncing in my room wearing next to nothing. "You girls can't come upstairs. Roger and I will be having sex," she proudly announced.

I gasped and my friends stared at me with wide eyes. No one said anything. I was embarrassed and disgusted beyond belief that she had just announced this in front of them. "So, let's just go back to playing Barbies," I said. Everyone shook their heads, grabbed their barbies, and we went back to playing as if nothing I had happened.

She always had to find a way to be the center of attention, and she seemed jealous of our joy.

It became even more evident to me that attention was like oxygen to her. It was more than just a need for attention, though. Something more bizarre appeared to be going on. When Mom danced, she'd invite my friends to get up and dance with her, yet, she'd never allowed me to participate, completely excluding me from being part of the fun.

This emerging pattern of excluding me began to show up in other strange ways. Sometimes after spending the weekend with Dad, I would come home and discover my friends already in the house hanging out with Mom. She's pre-arranged a sleepover but made sure my friends came over long before she knew I would be home. She proceeded to hang out with my friends while they waited for me, insisting on showing them a great time.

*Why was she doing hanging out with **MY** friends?*

One day, I came home to find that she had orchestrated an elaborate tea party for my friends. She made a big production of pouring grape juice into fancy glasses, acting as if it was wine. But, just as she did with her over-the-top karaoke dancing sessions, I was never allowed to partake. Whether it was grape juice, brownies, or candy, Mom would taunt me.

"Don't these brownies smell delicious?" Mom smirked at me and took a bite of her brownie. "Mmmm-mmm, they taste SO good. Don't you agree girls?" She'd say to my friends.

My friends ate the brownies but gave me a look of uncertainty before staring back at Mom and replying in agreement with smiles and sounds of delight.

Are you kidding me? Is this a joke?

I shook my head and peered at my mom. "Can I have one?" I'd ask.

"You can't have any. They are just for us." She'd point back and forth between herself and my friends. I swallowed hard, feeling jealous of the love my friends were receiving from Mom. Not being served a brownie or a glass of grape juice confirmed my feelings of disconnection as Mom's daughter.

Why would she do a tea party for random people but not for me?

Why am I omitted?

Why are my friends playing along?

What did I do wrong?

Does anyone else see how strange this is?

I could tell that Mom was capable of being playful and nurturing, and kids enjoy fun and games like what Mom made for my friends. But, then why was I left out and why couldn't she do these things for me?

Mom continued making a distinct effort to leave me out. It was almost as if she enjoyed seeing me upset and crying. When I would cry, she would never console me. She often had a smirk of satisfaction in the wake of my humiliation.

When she did engage with the business of parenting, it was almost comical. If we needed to go anywhere, we'd have to ask neighbors or friends to take us because mom didn't have a driver's license. Mom decided that *now* would be the time to get one, and that created a lot of internal worry within me about what would happen next with her having a license. She was a terrible driver and on multiple occasions, put us in danger while she was behind the wheel.

Every siren and sound panicked her in a way that I didn't understand. She also had a deathly fear of the snow. She'd never drive in it, but this was Utah, and it snowed a lot in the winter. On the moments where she had to drive in the snow, she'd make a huge production out of it, biting her nails down, hyperventilating, and shaking as if her body was going through shock. I couldn't tell if it was an act or if something was really wrong with her. I'd help direct her to the side of the road. It annoyed me. How did she not know this? It became increasingly embarrassing to have her act like a child, and intensely overwhelming to be in the adult role as a kid.

Mom was the talk around town about many things, but her driving had become increasingly gossip worthy after she crashed the car into a tree while taking a bunch of my friends and I to school. Another time, she had Trina and Trent in the car and ran over a fire hydrant because she thought a bee was in the car with her. I heard all about it when I got a slip to come to the main office. Mom called me at school to let me know what had happened and informed me that she couldn't pick me up from school that day. Later, I heard from multiple people that they actually witnessed seeing Mom drag the fire hydrant behind her car. After that, no one let their kids drive anywhere with Mom. She could not be trusted behind the wheel.

Over time, my friends made excuses about why they couldn't come play with me. When I asked them about it, they would mention that their parents didn't want them coming to my house anymore because of my home situation. At times, I'd go knock on the door at my friend's house.

"Hi Tiffany." Shauntal's Mom said.

"Hey. Can Shauntal play?" I'd ask.

Her Mom paused. "Are you going to play in the front yard or go to your house? Cause if you're going to play outside, play outside, but she's not allowed to go over to your house." I felt embarrassed and alienated.

These incidents pained me in a different way than the physical abuse. Mom's behavior was also creating a rift with my friendships because their parents didn't trust her. It was times like these that created more distance between us. These incidents seared themselves into my memory and the emotional heartbreak grew immensely.

At the same time as my relationship with Mom was taking this new strange turn, her relationship with Roger was beginning to nosedive.

A perfect storm was brewing.

In the past, Roger would never physically hit Mom or us kids. Instead, he would use his strange form of psychological torture to exact punishment. However, as time passed, something had shifted in Roger, and whatever iron control he had exerted over his darker impulses was beginning to slip away from him. Now, his fights with Mom became physically violent.

On a Saturday afternoon, I was down in my bedroom, and I could hear Mom and Roger yelling at each other. I got used to their constant fights, and went about my business, until I heard a large thudding crash from upstairs. It sounded as if the entertainment center fell to the floor.

What's going on?

Is everyone okay?

I was nervous about what I would find as I crept up the stairs. My anxiety pulsed through my shaking hands. I took a deep breath at the top of the staircase and peered through the railing to gaze around the room.

I gasped.

Mom cried as she laid crumpled against the wall.

She's hurt.

My heart sank for Mom. Her body was turned toward me, and I could see an eggshell size bump on her forehead that resembled something out of a cartoon. Except this was no cartoon. This was reality.

Roger was nowhere.

Where are Trent and Trina?

My heart thrashed through my chest, beating way too fast. I scoured the room but couldn't see them. I yelled their names as I raced through each room, without any response.

Opening the door, I went outside and found them in the back, playing in our fenced yard.

How did Trina get down the stairs?

Running to them, I pulled them into a hug. "Are you okay?" I asked. Trent nodded back to me, just as sirens blared down our street. I placed my hands over my ears, showing them to mimic me. Trina was two and liked to copy what I did, and Trent followed my lead. They covered their ears, just as the paramedics pulled up in front of our house. Our neighbor who lived on the south side of us, could see through our chain link fence that connected our backyard to her side yard. Through all the commotion going on, she came over to examine what was going on and I left Trina and Trent with her, while I ran in to see what was going on with Mom.

The paramedics made their way into the house and helped Mom with her wounds. "How did this happen?"

I overheard Mom explaining that Roger had pushed her into the wall, followed by several kicks while he wore combat boots. "We were fighting, and he hit me," she said.

After the paramedics cleaned Mom up and heard her account of what took place, they called the police to report a domestic violence incident.

I worried for my younger siblings about what they may have seen, if they were hurt, and I wanted to get them away from the situation quickly. We were sent over to stay with the neighbors as the police interviewed Mom.

I was happy to have my siblings with me, where I knew they were okay. I climbed in the neighbor's tree, my safe place, while Trent and Trina played on the grass below me. I could see them, and they could see me. When the ambulance pulled away from our house, I watched it drive in the distance, wondering if Mom was alright.

When would Roger be back?

Would we be bouncing again?

Our neighbor kept us until Mom got back home from the hospital.

After that episode, I was always scared around Roger. I now knew what he was capable of. Being around him felt like being around a ticking time bomb that could go off at any moment. Back in our home, things were changing. Before, when Mom and Roger would fight, he'd kick Mom and us kids out of the house. Now, when they fought, Roger would leave—sometimes for days, sometimes longer. When Roger stormed off, we would never know when or if he would come back.

My stomach cramped and I got nauseated often. I couldn't sleep wondering if Roger would hurt me and my siblings, like he did Mom.

Every noise jarred me as made my body went into freeze mode preparing for when and if Roger came home. I felt uncertain and unprepared for the explosion that awaited. It seemed like it was only a matter of time.

Roger planned on becoming a firefighter, but his applications got rejected because of the domestic violence charge on his record from what he did to Mom. That was one of the only good things to come out of what Roger did.

One evening, I was down in my basement bedroom—part of which was still unfinished— when I heard strange noises in the middle of the night. It sounded like *something* was down there with me, messing with the door handle.

Was it a ghost or an intruder?

I constantly felt on guard and afraid, especially at night. I grabbed Trent from his bedroom, which was next to mine, and we ran as fast as we could upstairs to Mom's room, where she stayed with Trina. Mom could also hear loud noises which resembled someone banging on pipes and smacking walls. She told us to stay quiet but was panicking which added to my nerves. I didn't want the noise she was making to tell the intruder where we were. I normally calmed her down, but this time I couldn't as my body froze. My stomach gurgled and I needed to go to the bathroom, but I didn't want to race across the hall and have someone catch me.

I'm going to die.

I closed my eyes and held my stomach, trying to keep still.

Mom grabbed the phone and quickly called the police to report a prowler. I shook and could barely breathe as we huddled together in Mom's bedroom. The strange banging sound below, had a pattern of multiple hits at a time. There would be a pause long enough for me to think that it was over, only for the beats to come back taunting me once again. We listened and stared at each other, desperately waiting for the police to arrive. Time felt like it stood still as the uncertainty of the situation took hold.

After what seemed like an eternity, the police barged through the door, letting us know they had arrived. With flashlights and guns drawn, they went down into the basement. There they discovered the "prowler" under the stairwell.

Roger.

He'd snuck into the unfinished basement through the separate entry and hid down there.

The police couldn't arrest him because he technically lived in the house, not to mention the house was in his name, to begin with.

Why would he do something like that?

I didn't fully understand what he was trying to do.

This was just another added spotlight on me that made me stand out from my peers, in a way that I didn't want to be known for. I already had been a spotlight kid from bouncing around all the time. This continual police visits didn't help with school gossip. I wanted to be invisible. I worried that if Mom or I went down to the basement to confront him during his little "attacks," he might have a knife or something worse. Who knew what he was capable of or what he would do next? This was not normal behavior.

Roger seemed to love to scare and taunt us as he continued his strange "break-ins," finding new ways to sneak into the basement without us knowing it, as if he were on a mission to make us feel under attack. He'd also sneak into the house during the day when we were away and leave little mementos to let us know he'd been there. Roger claimed he'd tap the phone when he moved out, so he'd be aware of everything we were saying. It became such an unnerving environment. It was like living in a dark thriller.

As scared as we were during those moments, even scarier was the underlying sense that Roger was slowly becoming unhinged.

a storm is brewing

ONE THING MOM LIKED about me was that, in her eyes, I was a handy servant to have around, or at least that's what she said. She and Roger had gone ahead and had another baby a few years after Trina was born—this time a baby boy named Troy. Mom loved her "T" names. Now, she had three kids to look after while Roger was away at work. Whenever she wanted to take off, which was often, she would order me to watch Trent(5), Trina(2) and Troy, who was newly born.

I was eleven.

She'd leave to go gambling or to visit one of her boyfriends. I was available, but more importantly, she didn't need to pay me.

One day, Trent and I returned from spending time with Dad. I walked into a quiet house which was abnormal from the regular loud and static sounds we'd typically hear when we arrived. My siblings Trina, and Troy usually would be vocal, Mom would've had the TV on to watch one her favorite shows, or there would be arguing, but it was silent. I took Trent's hand and we stepped into the house, moving toward the kitchen. From around the corner, I could see Trina. As I walked into the kitchen, Troy held a butcher knife in his hand. He was in a diaper and had a yellow substance all over his body.

I jumped. "No Troy. Give that to me."

Moving quickly toward him, I carefully took the knife from his hand, and placed it away from him so he couldn't reach it again.

Why are they alone?

They could've hurt each other.

"Mom?" I yelled. "Where are you?"

The silence let me in on the fact that she wasn't there and had left Trina and Troy alone to fend for themselves.

"Troy. What's all over your body?" I asked.

He gazed down at the ground and pointed to a mustard bottle. I grabbed a washcloth from a kitchen drawer and soaked it in warm water from the sink. My hands shook wringing the cloth out. I turned off the faucet and bent down to be eye level with Troy. As I gently wiped the mustard off his body, there was a knock at the door. I carried Troy with me, and Trina and Trent followed.

I opened the door to a very frantic neighbor staring at me. "Are you okay? Have you been here the whole time?"

"What? No, I just got home." I said.

She held her head. "I just called the police. About fifteen minutes ago, I saw Troy running outside in a diaper and yellow paint all over him. I couldn't see your mom and got concerned. Is she home?"

I swallowed and shook my head.

"They've been here without you or your mom?" Her voice raised an octave higher.

I nodded and couldn't bring myself to stare at her.

After that, I began having heightened anxiety about not being close to my younger siblings when I was away with Dad.

Only by the grace of God did my siblings not hurt himself, but what if it happened again.

Would they be that lucky a second time? What would I come home to?

At school, fear stood in place of focus, as not only did I worry about Roger and Mom's behavior, but the safety of my siblings, too. My anxiety around these feelings turned into panic when I came home from school to Mom screaming and pacing the kitchen.

I put my backpack on the floor. "What's wrong, Mom?"

She stared at me with wide eyes. "The kids got into the medicine and took my pills. I need to call an ambulance."

"How did this happen?" I asked. "Where were you?"

Mom stared at the ground, ignoring me, and called 911. My siblings were conscious and appeared fine, but my fear told me different stories.

They're going to die.

What if they're not okay?

I'm going to lose my siblings.

This seems very bad.

The pills shouldn't have been out in the first place or in a spot where they could reach them. They were too little to understand that it wasn't candy. When the ambulance came, Trina and Troy were rushed to the hospital to have their stomachs pumped.

That didn't change anything for Mom. She kept leaving and doing the same things over and over again. Her number one priority was her own pleasure—whether that was men, sex, money, drugs, or gambling. My siblings and I appeared to be at the bottom of the list.

My understanding of the world was changing and growing, and as I got older, I began to see Mom more clearly. I viewed things with a little more perspective. I started to see Mom in a clear light for what she was, and that shift was a painful experience. It made the pain of the physical abuse in some ways worse. I began to understand that she should know better than to behave this way and Mom should be able to see the depth of how wrong her actions were.

I noticed a lot more things, like the fact that Mom never picked up a book. Not one, ever. She could never be bothered to fill out forms and would have me sign documents for her, whether they were license and job applications, my school parent permission forms, or court documents. I even wrote a few court documents for Mom in regard to a child support and custody hearing. True, mom had horrible handwriting, but she could learned to write if she had wanted to. Like other things, it was just a case of her being lazy and having someone else do the dirty work for her. These little things I saw and experienced, were important as they continued to show and give me awareness that I wasn't my mother. I could be different if I chose to be.

These little pivot points started to allow me to grow up and move out of her shadow.

Even though most of the extreme bouncing from when we had lived in Salt Lake City had ended, there were times when Mom would pack us kids up once again to stay with my grandparents in order to get away from Roger. We thought we were safe being far away from him.

How wrong we were.

Once, when Mom and Roger were on a break again, we were at church when my siblings acted up during the services, so I volunteered to entertain them out into the foyer. I knew Mom was going to assign me the task anyway, as she did often. I held Troy, in my lap while we waited for Mom and Grammie to come out of services.

Next thing I know, Roger came through the church doors, and quickly walked toward me.

What is Roger doing here?

My shoulders tightened in response to my internal thought.

Roger pulled Troy from my lap, grabbed Trina by the arm, and took off. He didn't say a word, just simply snatched them. It all happened so quickly. He was gone faster than I could react, like one of those slow-motion moments when you want to act, but you can't. I was so blindsided that I froze, unable to move.

When Mom and Grammie came to the foyer, I pointed to the door. "Rrrrrog…" I stuttered, trying to get his name out. "Took kids."

Mom stepped forward. "What do you mean Roger took the kids? Why did you let that happen? You should've come to get me."

"I . . . don't know." My body shook the more she shamed me for losing sight of my siblings. I lost them and it was all my fault. I didn't protect them like I wanted to. Mom labeled me as the "screw up" and the "bad kid" for not somehow stopping Roger.

Once again, Roger had gotten away with another sneak attack, and once again, the police said there was nothing they could do about it. Roger was their dad and he had joint custody with Mom. Despite Mom's harsh accusation, I tried to shake it off, but that event weighed heavily on my conscience, and I did blame myself.

After the church incident, when my siblings came back home, the episodes with Roger continued. I was at my grandparents' house with Grandpa and Trent. Mom and Grammie wanted to run an errand and went for a drive with Trina and Troy. A while later, we heard the car engine in the carport, and car doors slamming quickly. A frantic energy moved through the kitchen as Mom, Grammie, Trina, and Troy rushed into the back door of the house.

What's going on?

Grandpa stood up quickly and went right over to them.

"He came out of nowhere." Mom began recounting in panic how Roger showed up out of nowhere, driving alongside them, and tried to run them off the road. When Grammie eventually pulled over, Roger stopped next to them and got out of his car, demanding the children be given over to him. Grammie explained that they refused his demand, and Roger reached through the window, trying to strangle Grammie.

Even after these multiple incidents and even though Roger mistreated Mom, the strings were always attached, and she could never cut that tie. There was a time when I went downstairs to go to my room and found Mom in Travis' room sitting against the wall, crying and holding a knife to her neck. "My life is over without Roger, Tiffany. I'll kill myself if he doesn't come back."

I sat with her and held her hand. "What are you talking about, Mom? This isn't the end of your life. You can do something about it. This isn't the way."

She put the knife down and sobbed, while I sat by her until I knew it was over.

Amidst all of the things that I had to be mad about in my life, and there were many, the fact that Mom wouldn't leave Roger frustrated and perplexed me more than anything else.

Sometimes, it even consumed my thoughts so heavily that it would distract me from school.

Why doesn't she leave?

Why doesn't she stand up for herself?

To me, there was something sadly wrong with this picture. It was odd how I found myself switching roles from child to parent quite often with Mom. Even though I was only in sixth grade, I constantly urged her to leave Roger. I explained to her that she could survive without a man, especially without Roger. Even so, it felt like my advice fell on deaf ears. No matter what I said, she never saw it my way.

I held a lot of anger inside for the longest time towards Mom. Witnessing the pain, she put herself through with Roger due to her lack of confidence had the result of making me want to strive to be everything she wasn't.

That's not going to happen to me. I won't let it.

I knew the person and idea of what I wanted to become was the opposite of anything like Mom. She'd never done anything to make a positive impression on me. Mom's capitulation to her situation struck a chord deep inside me. For some reason, I knew that everyone had a burning flame inside themselves, even someone like Mom—for all her faults— still had some fire inside her. She had a potential to do good things and be happy. What really bothered me more than anything else was that she didn't see it in herself. She refused to grasp her own potential and light her flame within. Instead, she allowed herself to become a *victim*.

Inside me, I already knew I was different than her. I promised myself to be a better person. I knew there was something strong inside me— inside all of us— that's bigger than our circumstances. None of us ever had to be a prisoner to the situation we were currently in. We all had the power to light our flame within.

Little did I know how hard I would soon be fighting to keep that flame burning as big and bright as it needed to be, in order to survive.

the cabin

WHEN I WAS ELEVEN, we would often go on camping trips with family and friends to a small area in Price, Utah, a modest drive about two hours southeast of Salt Lake City. Roger was especially fond of Price, mainly because he'd built a rustic cabin there with his father when he was a teenager. Price held special memories for Roger in spending time with his dad. We'd often stay at the cabin on the weekends with family friends of Rogers; most often, Carla, Don, and their kids would accompany us.

I wasn't the biggest fan of camping, but I enjoyed the journey getting there. We would pile into the back of one of the pick-up trucks. If it were daytime, we'd entertain ourselves during the ride by playing the license plate game, or we'd make up songs. We each would take turns singing "Ice, Ice Baby," by Vanilla Ice, and see who could rap the whole way through without stopping or making mistakes. If we were driving at night, we'd all lie down in the bed of the truck, in our sleeping bags to stargaze, shouting and pointing out constellations as they appeared one by one in the big sky night overhead.

The cabin that Roger and his father had built was extremely rustic. It was a shell of a place, run-down, and a gathering spot for a few odd pieces of furniture here and there that people didn't want anymore. There was a table, a few chairs, and a couch, but beds and nightstands were vacant. Mom and Roger had the only bed in the place, and everyone else slept on mattresses sprawled across the floor. It wasn't insolated, and the reddish-brown wood took the place of drywall. We had no running water, electricity, telephone service, or bathroom. All of our food and supplies came with us for the weekend. The adults would build a big fire in the fireplace, which was our main source of heat and light for the whole time we were there. It was a stunning location, nestled in a beautiful Aspen Forest high up in the Wasatch Mountains. I loved the stream that flowed a few feet down, and the pine trees that towered above us, giving off a fresh aroma. My favorite, though—the stars. Because there were no city lights, we could see so many up in the mountains. The sky felt infinite and magical. Here, I could think about the good in the world and about possibilities as I watched shooting stars.

Truthfully, though, I always dreaded going to that cabin.

For one, I had an overactive imagination, and being in the middle of nowhere without a telephone or another house in sight absolutely terrified me. I freaked myself out with endless "what if" scenarios. I would lie on the floor of the dark cabin at night, desperately wanting to fall asleep as quickly as possible. I was convinced if I stayed up and peered out the window into the dark woods, I would see the outline of a monster staring back at me attempting to come inside to snatch me up. Every sound scared me into wondering what may be lurking outside the cabin.

The other scenario I worried about often was what to do if someone got hurt while we were up there.

How would we call for help?

What if the car wouldn't start?

How would we get back home?

I didn't like the sense of being so isolated and cut off from the rest of the world.

One time, Mom and Roger got into a fight at the cabin. In a rage, Roger got into his truck and sped off, leaving us alone. We weren't sure if he'd come back, and I was panicked as my mind wandered even deeper into my fears.

What are we going to do?

How are we going to get down the mountain?

What if he doesn't come back?

He eventually did come back, but after that it became hard to ignore the fact that I didn't trust my mom or stepfather. My fear escalated being in the woods and I never felt at ease. It didn't take much to set my imagination off down a dark path of no return.

One afternoon we were out exploring in the woods when we came across a dried-up riverbed. There was a bunch of old rotting cars. I, of course, immediately thought the worse. What if there were skeletons from a car crash that no one had ever found? I cringed at the thought of the rotting bodies before my mind jumped to a more heightened scenario.

What if the people survived the initial accident but then was attacked and killed by some ferocious animal?

What if that same vicious beast was out in the woods right now, watching us, stalking its next prey?

I worked myself up into an absolute tizzy.

Don, the family friend who often accompanied us on these trips, was an old friend of Rogers. I never had a good feeling about Don. He was a heavy-set man with long cropped hair and yellowish teeth.

He was kind of greasy, and the jeans he always wore looked like he had been wearing them for days. I got the sense that Don didn't shower too often, but it's what Don did to me in the dark of night that made me genuinely fear him.

At night all the kids would spread out their sleeping bags across the cabin floor while the adults slept upstairs in a loft. One night, I woke up and found Don right next to me. I was very confused, unsure what he was doing there. Don proceeded to molest me sexually. While everyone else in the cabin slept, Don began to rub his hands all over me. I stayed frozen with fear. Nothing like this had ever happened to me before. I breathed in his rank body odor as he proceeded to perform oral sex on me. As he does it, I'm shaking. Even though people are close by, I'm too scared to shout out for someone to do something. It was like having a waking nightmare. When he finally leaves me to go back to his sleeping bag, I feel gross and used. I sunk into my sleeping bag and began to cry as quietly as possible.

What just happened??

The following day, everyone got up like it was just another day. As they all go about their business, I tried to understand what occurred with Don in my sleeping bag. I still can't quite believe what happened the night before *actually* happened. I'm baffled about what Don did to me. I wonder why anyone would put their mouth where Don put his on me. It felt wrong and dirty. He violated me, but I didn't know how to process it. I convinced myself that it was a bad dream.

Maybe, if I didn't say anything, it would all just go away. I said nothing. I didn't tell Mom or Roger what happened to me, and it didn't just go away, nor did it turn out to be a bad dream.

Don started making regular advances during our frequent weekend trips to the cabin.

He'd take all the kids to the local swimming hole for a swim. While the other kids splashed around and frolicked, Don would stay close to me in the water, making his way with his fingers into my bathing suit underwater so that no one could see what he was doing. Don would also grab my hand under the water and place it on his privates, moving my hand back and forth.

That was the first time I had ever touched a man's penis. I wanted to throw up, and I wanted it to stop, but I was scared of the consequences if I did anything. His behavior became a persistent part of our family visits to the cabins. It got so bad that I dreaded the weekends because I knew what was in store for me.

I tried to stay with a friend over those cabin weekends, so I didn't have to go, or tell Mom and Roger that I didn't feel well. My stomach hurt a lot with worry. I tried to get out of going, but it never worked. Instead, they'd use my fear against me. Taunting me.

"Quit being a baby."

"What's that behind you in the woods?"

"Did you hear that noise?"

The burden of keeping the secret of what Don was doing became too much to bear. It was not just the sense of violation and disgust that flowed over me every time he touched me. It was also the *weight* of keeping it all inside. I could no longer deny what was really happening, and that what he was doing was wrong, absolutely wrong. No one was going to stop him unless I said something. It was a scary proposition, but after six months, I worked up all my courage and told Mom and Roger about Don touching me. Being faced with the prospect of another weekend with Don was too much to continue to hold. It was a huge relief to tell them at the cabin, and finally let this dark secret I'd been carrying around with me out into the open. I was convinced that my work was done, and I had hoped Mom would step forward to protect her daughter.

Much to my surprise, they didn't believe me. I stood there next to Don when they confronted him with what I had told them. Mom and Roger asked him about the accusations, and he denied it all. He said nothing happened and that I was "making it all up." Mom and Roger shook their heads.

"You both can't be telling the truth," Mom said.

Instead of Mom taking my word, her own flesh and blood, she believed Don. Mom and Roger then proceeded to try and convince me that I was making it all up.

"You always have had overactive imagination." They said. "You get spooked easy."

Are you kidding me?

As Mom and Roger wrote off my cry for help as just silly ramblings, I experienced a new kind of pain and confusion. It's different than the physical pain and revulsion that I had experienced while Don was molesting me.

I did the right thing.

I found the courage to come forward, and most importantly, I had the truth on my side. Yet, Don was getting away with it.

How can that be?

How can my mother, who is supposed to be on my side, not believe me?

Being molested was painful. Being betrayed by those you count on to protect you was something far worse.

The weather turned cold, and the camping trips came to an end for that year. Don was out of my life for now. The sexual encounters with Don were over, and I no longer had to dread the weekend the cabin visits.

innocence lost

AS I STARTED EIGHTH GRADE, our family moved to a new house that my siblings and I referred to as "The Brown House," which described our brick home. As with the blue house in West Jordan, Mom and Roger were able to get a great deal by buying a house in foreclosure. The Brown House was a five bedroom, three bath home, much bigger and newer than our old house. It was a rambler with a fireplace, hot tub, and a completely finished basement. All things that we never had at the blue home. Our bedrooms were significantly larger, and we had a fenced-in yard. I even had MY own bathroom. It didn't have its own entrance downstairs, which made me feel safe because then Roger didn't have access to lurk in and bang on the pipes to torment us again like he did in the blue house. I spent the summer babysitting and doing jobs around the neighborhood so I could buy myself a Nintendo system. I was determined. When I *finally* got my own Nintendo, my friends would come over, and we'd play in the family room, which was right outside my bedroom. It was cozy and away from everyone else. I liked that.

Trent and I had our rooms in the basement, and Troy and Trina's rooms were upstairs near Mom and Roger. Each of our rooms had a wallpaper border with a theme. I'd never had that before and I thought only rich people experienced this kind of upgrade. Trent had the "football" room, and I had the "cat" room. Trina's room was embellished with Minnie Mouse and Troy's walls were a nice shade of baby blue. We were all excited to be living there as this felt like a major step up! I also continued to take private viola lessons that Roger had been paying for. I took the classes with Ester Larsen. She was very well known in the community and her daughter played for the Utah Symphony. Ester recommended that I get into Viola competitions, called Federation. I agreed that I would like to try and began practicing for hours a day on the musical pieces that I would compete with. Competitions typically fell on the Saturdays that we were with Dad. He had us every other weekend.

I had to dress nice for the competitions and that excited me.

I begged Dad to get me some pantyhose. "Please Dad. Can we go to the store?" Dad gazed at me with no expression on his face and paused. *Did he hear me? Did he understand what this means to me?*

I stared at him. "This is important to me. Please, Dad."

"Okay, we can do that." *Yes!*

I smiled.

I had never had a pair of pantyhose before. Dad and I took the bus to Walmart to get me pantyhose for my outfit, and then we took multiple buses to get up to the University of Utah where the Federations were held. I felt like I had entered womanhood with this purchase, both fancy and grown-up. I had to memorize the seven-page composition and work on keeping my hands steady as I played. I got judged on intonation, bow stroke, and vibrato. It helped me to have confidence in my ability to work and create under pressure, but I also learned how to take constructive criticism. As I peered down the halls and soaked in the energy of where I was. I dreamed of one day being part of the Universities Symphony, the Utah Philharmonic. This was something that I loved to do because of the sense of accomplishment I felt and being recognized for my hard work. It also kept my mind off the current situation at home.

The Brown House coincided with Mom's relationship with Roger, declining to new lows. Roger would mess with us by playing psychological games more often, and his favorite seemed to be ignoring us intentionally for days, even weeks on end. The behavioral torture of the silent treatment took on another level and he became more volatile than ever before. All of us lived in fear of him, not knowing what he could or would do. It was a really weird time for me as Mom and Roger would fight more often and I could feel the tension. I didn't like that, but we weren't bouncing from place to place anymore and there wasn't on and off separation encounters. That felt more secure.

I established friendships in a way that I hadn't allowed myself to do before, and I started letting my guard down and setting roots.

At the same time, entering puberty elicited new forms of psychological abuse from Mom.

These physical changes in me were also affecting Roger.

One night, Roger and Mom had a tickle fight with me in their upstairs bedroom, mostly Roger tickled the two of us. It lasted about an hour, and we were all laughing, a rare moment that I appreciated.

Mom and Roger were being playful. This is nice.

"Take her to bed," Mom said whimsically to Roger.

Roger put me over his shoulder and carried me down to my bedroom in the basement as I continued to laugh.

Things can be different for me.

He plopped me down on my bed, and then to my surprise, he didn't leave. He just stood in the doorway staring at me. His eyes were cold, sinister, and calculated, as if he was forming an evil plan—waiting.

It scared me.

I held my breath and sucked my hope back in.

I'd never seen a man look at me like that before with such lust and wanting. When Don stared at me, it was as if he saw me as a kid. This was different with Roger, and I could feel it in my body as chills ran up my arms. To break the tension, I got up and began to clean my room. Roger continued to watch me silently.

I felt very awkward, feeling his eyes on me, not knowing what to do or how to make him leave. Eventually, I turned to Roger. "What?"

He said nothing in reply but kept peering at me with a leering smirk on his face. Roger waited for a few more minutes, then he turned and left without saying a word.

The next morning, I was lying in bed, not wanting to get up for school. I was still half asleep and opened my eyes just barely when I felt the water shift strangely under the sheets of my waterbed. It took me a second to process my surroundings, but when I did, I quickly closed my eyes, pretending I was asleep. Roger sat on the bed next to me.

My hands began perspiring.

How do I get out of this?

He's too big to push away.

What do I do?

Do I scream?

Who's going to listen and protect me if I scream?

He bent down and kissed me on my mouth, moving his tongue along my lips. I could taste the foulness of cigarettes and coffee on his breath. I wanted to gag, but I was too terrified to move, so I just tried to continue acting like I was still sleeping. I feel helpless.

What's happening?

Why's he doing this?

This is wrong.

I wasn't sure how much time had passed, but it felt like forever. Eventually, Roger stopped kissing me. Without saying a word, he got up and left the room. I laid in bed and sobbed, in shock from what Roger had done to me. A little while later, I got up and scrubbed my mouth with toothpaste and Listerine multiple times to get the taste of cigarettes off my tongue and lips.

I'm disgusted and my stomach ached. I wanted to go to school and be on time, because it was important to me. I took a deep breath and hesitantly walked upstairs, every step quieter than the one before.

Did Roger leave for work?

Is he up there?

Please don't let him be here.

Mom was there.

So was Roger.

I froze and my stomach clenched tighter.

What do I do?

He said nothing, grabbed his coffee, and left for work just as he does every morning. Our normal morning ritual of getting ready for school commenced as if nothing had happened.

Maybe I should tell Mom?

I wanted to reach out to her, but she didn't support me with Don. Why would she listen and believe me now?

After breakfast, I go downstairs to shower. I try to scrub Roger's scent from my skin. I sob in the glass stall as the hot water runs over me, wondering what just happened. I made my way to school, and walked through the halls like a zombie, trying to process what took place that morning.

For the next few days, when I was forced to be alone with Roger, I'm on guard for whatever he may try, and I've grown worried about any time I have to spend time alone with him. My best strategy was to stay at friends' houses and not come home. Nothing else happened, and I feel like the incident wasn't existent. I say nothing to Mom or my friends at school.

Why would Roger do something like that to me?

I don't want to think about it, and I hope it will go away and never happen again.

A week later, Roger picks me up from my symphony practice. We're driving in his Blazer as we got stopped at a red light.

"You're sexy. Did you know that?" he said.

I looked at him. "*What did he just say?*"

I didn't know how to respond, so I just stared out the window praying for God to please change the light to green so I can get out of there. I said it over and over in my head. That light seemed like the longest traffic light I'd ever been stopped at in my life.

Finally, the light turns green, and we began driving again.

He continued. "Well, you are. You turn me on."

I can't even begin to know what to say to him. I moved closer to the passenger side door, holding my arms, and continued staring out the window. I didn't want to look at him. The streets of Salt Lake City pass by, and I'm scared to think about where he might be taking me. It's almost as if Roger can hear my thoughts. "We're going to go shopping. I want to buy you something nice," he said.

Why?

The last time he bought me something nice was when we first moved in, and I got a gum ball machine.

What's he up to now?

Roger pulled into the K-mart parking lot. He took my hand, guiding me into the store and we walked straight to the jewelry counter. He pointed out a locket under the locked glass and asked if I would like it.

I liked to shop.

I thought the necklace was pretty.

He peered at me with a questionable look. "So, do you like it?"

There were other people around, so I was starting to feel a bit safer.

In a low voice, I nodded. "Yes, I like it."

Roger told the saleswoman behind the counter that we'll take it. He bought the necklace for me, and we left the store with it around my neck. We got back in the Blazer and Roger turned toward me. "If your Mom or anyone else asks where you got the necklace, tell them a boy at school bought it for you."

I cleared my throat and looked in his direction, but not directly at him. "Why?"

"Your Mom would get mad at me for spending so much money on a necklace for you."

He said, "It's just better for all of us this way."

Gripping the locket around my neck, I nodded.

He started the car and drove towards home.

Part of me hoped that the locket was the end of it and that he was using it to buy my silence for a one-time incident. The early morning encounters begin again a couple of days after the necklace purchase. Roger came into my bedroom before anyone else was awake and touched me as part of what would become a sick and twisted morning "routine." As with the first incident, I always pretended to be asleep. Each time it was the same. He kissed and rubbed on my breasts while I laid there before he eventually left without ever saying a word. These encounters became almost a daily thing. The days he didn't visit me in the early dawn were rarer than the days he did.

After one of Roger's visits, I took a hot shower to try and scrub myself clean of him. While rinsing the shampoo out of my hair, I got an eerie sensation all over my body. I wiped the water away from my eyes. Through the steamed shower door, I saw a silhouette in the doorway of the bathroom.

It was Roger.

He was watching me shower.

I felt like an animal on display. It made my skin crawl, and I was nauseous and weak. I had nowhere to run or go.

I was terrified of Roger, and I pretended that no one was there while I quickly continued with the rest of my shower. I was overcome with a mix of revulsion, anger, and fear seeing the lust in his eyes. Roger finally left to go upstairs to get ready for work. As time progresses, Roger tried to push the envelope, going a little farther with me each time. I didn't know how to put a stop to it. It seemed to be spiraling out of control, and I didn't know where it would end. Soon, the sexual abuse spread beyond just our early morning routine. He began to create pockets of time when just the two of us were alone in the house. This meant the charade of me being asleep and unaware of what he was doing, now goes by the wayside. Roger knew that I was fully awake and aware of what he was doing. He made sure to tell me that if I told anyone, ANYONE AT ALL, he'd KILL me. I took his threats seriously as I believed he could follow through with the psychological and emotional torture I'd seen from him with us in the past. Roger was a strong man with a dark side. I was just a growing young girl, meek and naïve.

How would I be able to fight him and protect myself?

I kept my mouth shut.

No one seemed to notice how Roger would go out of his way to arrange times for the two of us to be alone in the house together, especially Mom. Or at least she didn't show any sign of knowing because surely, she'd say something if she did, or would she? I didn't understand how no one could see. It was maddening to me. There were times I'd be out babysitting when Roger called to say that I had to come home to do some chore or project. There was no chore or project, he'd make one up. Other times, we'd all be in the house, and he'd send Mom with my brothers and sister out on errands, yet say, "I needed to stay and do some homework." There were even moments I'd be at a friend's house, and when I called Mom to check-in, Roger would have her ask me to come home because he "needed my help with a few things."

I really don't want to go home.

Not this again.

I always felt terrified and helpless. I knew exactly what he was doing and what would come my way as soon as we were alone. There seemed to be nothing I could do to stop it.

The darkest moment came one weekend afternoon when Mom took my brothers and sister to a church function. I was lying on the floor in the living room watching TV, keeping to myself and minding my own business. Roger walked over, sat down next to me, and began to touch and feel my breasts.

Roger's never been this forward and aggressive before. This was different.

No. Please God. No.

My stomach turned over in knots. Roger told me to go into his bedroom and lay down on the bed.

I stood up, trying to move my shaking legs. I stared at the floor and held my shoulders, pretending that I didn't know where I was going even though my legs moved me there.

No. Don't go.

I was screaming inside, but I stayed quiet and slowly continued moving.

Roger followed me in. "Take off your pants."

I do as he said, but I left my panties on. Once I had my clothes off, he leaned over me and started French kissing me and touching me on top of my underwear. I could see his excitement, as his penis expanded through his pants. Roger undid his pants. He took them off and stood over me in his underwear and a T-shirt.

Roger began to kiss me again and rubbed his groin on my leg and stomach. He humped me over my underwear. I can't breathe and I'm frozen. It's as if I could understand what was going on, but I couldn't move. I was paralyzed and numb.

Get up.

Scream. Run.

I can't. He'll catch me.

Roger got more and more excited, and then he stopped for a moment. Walking over to his closet, Roger shuffled through a coat hanging in there. When he turned back to me, I saw that he was holding a condom and the darkness in his eyes showed me that he was somewhere else. I know what he was about to do. I'd never had sex before. I uncontrollably shook and cried as Roger walked back over to the bed.

He stood over me.

Get up.

My body was betraying me and not responding.

Tears ran down my face.

"Are you scared?" he asked.

I quickly nodded, unable even to speak.

"You don't want this do you?"

I shook my head as fast as I could.

Roger took a moment. "Don't worry, you will one day," he said, with an eerie look, "...Soon."

Roger headed back over to the closet where he put the condom away and left to go to the bathroom. I sat on the bed, still shaking. It felt like an earthquake had cracked within me, opening every part of my body. I was no longer whole. I felt broken. My body wasn't mine.

How did this happen? Why did this happen to me?

I quickly stood, got dressed and went down to my room. It was just the two of us in the house, and I was worried he might try again. If not today, then sometime soon—just as he said. Roger came down to my room a little while later, and my stomach tightened. There's no air filling my lungs.

Roger smiled. "If you tell your mom what happened today, I'll kill you." He peered at me with his cold stare. "Do you understand?"

I reluctantly nodded.

Roger didn't leave.

I held my shoulders and crossed my legs, in fear of what was going on in his head.

Is he going to try it again?

"I mean it," he said.

I knew he did.

Roger finally left. I closed my door, laid in my bed, and cried until I fell asleep.

CHAPTER THIRTEEN

leaving

NINE MONTHS PASSED SINCE that first episode on my waterbed. Roger still came down more mornings than not to have his way with me. I remain silent, terrified of the consequences of what would happen if I said anything.

At the end of the week, Roger came down to my room, woke me with kissing and fondling, and then left to work. Once he's gone, I began my ritual of getting ready for school and washing Roger off of me. One morning, Mom was up unusually early. After Roger left, she called me into her room and asked me why it took Roger so long to wake me up for school. My face felt warm as fear clouds my brain to search for an excuse.

"If you tell anyone, I'll kill you."

Roger's threats were still fresh in my mind. I didn't want to die, so I sputter something to Mom about Roger doing laundry while down in the basement with me that morning. I got dressed, and I was about ready to leave for school when Mom confronted me again. Mom had never really taken this kind of stock in my life. She checked downstairs and said there was no laundry in the washing machine or dryer. She asked me again what happened with Roger. I paused, not sure how to proceed. A flash of light cuts through the dark fear, and I realize this was my chance—I could end it.

Maybe this ONE time she'll protect me.

I agreed to myself quietly, and before I knew it, everything spilled out—everything that had happened with Roger since the tickle fights nine months ago. I told Mom about the necklace, the waterbed, and Roger's threats. As the words poured out of me, I felt a great weight of shame and fear lifting.

"What? I can't believe he did this." Mom flashed hot with rage. She's outraged. Her temper comes to a quick boil, only this time it was not directed at me. She called Roger at work and demanded that he came home immediately.

*Wait? What? She's **actually** defending me.*

I'd never seen her like that for me, so protective. She believed me and was on my side. I felt grateful, and I was in shock.

Mom informed me that I wasn't going to school as we were going to deal with this right then, as a family. We waited an hour or so for Roger to return. When Roger arrived, he announced that he wasn't happy about being disturbed at work. To him, it was all just a big inconvenience. Mom held her ground and confronted him with what I told her. As she went through the details, I sat and cried, staring at Roger with contempt and anger. When she was done, Mom asked Roger if any of it was true.

Roger looked up. "I did nothing."

Mom asked him again, demanding an answer.

"I did nothing." Roger didn't flinch and kept a straight face.

I can't believe that he lied to our faces. The anger inside me bubbled over, and my rage exploded as I ripped off the necklace that he bought me. I threw it at Roger and began to scream through my tears, "You're lying, and you know it!"

Roger sat there, cold as ice, doing nothing other than faking a few tears for a moment.

Once more, he told Mom that he did nothing.

Mom turned to me with a new look in her eyes, one that resembled dismissing me completely and turning off the care switch.

"Tiffany, are you sure this happened?"

How could Mom possibly believe that I would make something like this up? I froze with shock and aggression. I felt the callous of the situation suddenly shifting against me. The incident with Don from the family camping trip came flashing back. I'm reminded in that moment that Mom has never been without a man—EVER. She'll never be alone. It seemed to be hard-wired into her system to need a man's adoration and income. It appeared she was willing to sacrifice me for that need. Whatever maternal instincts that rose when faced with her husband sexually abusing her eldest child evaporate in the face of this deeper need of hers.

Her eyes grew darker, showing that her desires were taking over. The allegiances in the room switched. It was two against one, but now, I was left alone.

For a brief moment, I had a mother again.

Mom and Roger tried to make the whole incident go away, but they couldn't completely.

As a plea for help, I turned to a neighbor right across the street, who happened to be running for a state government position. She was my friend's mom. I told her what had been going on within my home. She reported our family to social services, and a new investigation opened. An interview was scheduled. I overheard Mom and Roger trying to figure out how to put the cat back in the bag. They offered me a later curfew, brand new basketball shoes, more sleepovers, a higher allowance—basically anything they could think of that I might want. They told me that all I had to do to get those things was to tell the state investigators that I was a good storyteller and that I made everything up.

The day of the interview arrived. Mom took me downtown to meet with the Department of Child and Family Services. Before I went into the room with the investigators, Mom put her arm around me and whispered, "Remember what we said. We'll give you all those things. All you have to do is tell them you made the whole thing up, ok? We love you."

Mom never said she loved me before, and where I knew there wasn't much truth to it, I held it for a while. Her arms wrapped around me felt nurturing and supportive. I didn't want it to go away, and I wanted her to keep holding me. I wanted Mom's love far more than any of the material things she and Roger were offering me. Even with all of the abuse and betrayal that I had endured, deep down, I still desperately hoped for things to be better between us. Here was my chance to finally get it. She was telling me how. When the investigators called me in, I told them that I was a good storyteller, just as my mother had asked me to.

That tender moment with Mom turned out, of course, to be a mirage. A few days after meeting with the DCFS investigators, Mom came down to my room in the basement, screaming,

"You have forty-eight hours to get the fuck out of my house." She didn't plan where I should go or what I should do, she just told me I had to leave. "Roger's given me a choice, you or him. I made my choice."

"How can you do this to your own flesh and blood?" I screamed. Anger, confusion, and fear crashed and stired inside me. This can't possibly be happening. I've done what they asked, and they're not delivering on their end of the promise. I've walked into a trap—a trap that was now about to leave me homeless and disregarded as Mom's child. My mother was about to kick her thirteen-year-old daughter out onto the street.

The next day, I went to school, still in a bit of shock, and officially checked out of my eighth-grade class. I went to every individual teacher to have them sign off that I had returned my schoolbooks. When the teachers asked me why I was checking out of school, I would stare down at my shoes and meekly say that I was moving. If I looked any of them in the eyes, I knew I would break down.

The whole process went very quickly. I didn't even really have a chance to say goodbye to any of my friends.

Walking home from school, I was at the top of the hill and I could see in the distance a bunch of people parked in front of my house. It appeared that people were coming and going from the yard, carrying items, one of which is my prized Huffy Bike.

Oh my gosh. Mom must have had a change of heart. We're moving! She's protecting me.

I smiled and got a little spring in my step and continued walking toward the house.

Wow.

Maybe I don't have to go. Mom's choosing me for once.

As I approached my house, I saw the items that people were carrying all looked very familiar to me.

They were my things.

They must be moving my room right now.

I paused.

Mom was in the front yard running a yard sale. It took me a few moments before I realized that the objects she was selling were my belongings. I stood there on the sidewalk . . . numb, staring as Mom sold my things right in front of me. I watched as another family took a box with my Nintendo and games, that I worked during the summer for. Mom sold it all for a mere ten dollars.

How could a mother sell her child's things?

I bunched my hands and my face flushed. The overriding sensation was a sickening realization that I was nothing to Mom.

I was disposable.

She was willing to *throw away* and disregard me without a second thought.

My life was over.

I stomped into the house and went down to my room, shocked by what I found waiting for me there. While Mom had been busy selling my stuff out front at the yard sale, Roger trashed my room. My pictures were crumpled up and ripped, and the remaining things that Mom didn't put up for sale outside were strewn all over the floor. It looked like a tornado had hit *only* my room.

I gathered what I could, toiletries and clothes mostly, and put them into a big black plastic garbage bag. I grabbed the little bit of cash I had stashed and saved up, hidden inside my Tootsie Roll bank. I went to my hiding spot to find the money was still there, somehow not found by Roger.

I counted it.

There were ten dollars to my name. I grabbed the garbage bag full of clothes and things, and I marched outside past Mom and her little yard sale. My heart dropped as I saw my siblings, and I slowly walked toward them. Placing my bag on the grass, I got down on their level, bringing them into a hug. "I love you guys. I've got to go for a while. Don't worry. Everything will be okay, I promise." I kissed them on their heads and stood.

Roger was nowhere. I never said goodbye to Mom, and she never bothered to chase after me and ask where I was going. I grabbed the garbage bag, left through the gate in the front yard and started to walk down the street to the local bus stop with NO clue where I'd be headed.

I silently cried making my way to the bus stop and continued looking behind me, waiting for someone, anyone, to come and rescue me and tell me this was just a bad dream.

No such luck.

I made my way to the bus stop. Oddly, I worried that people would think I was a transient because of my big black garbage bag. Eventually, the bus pulled up, and I used some of my money to buy a ticket into downtown Salt Lake City. The route going downtown ended, and I got off the bus.

It was early October and cold outside. I stared up at the tall buildings downtown as I walked around, trying to figure out where I was going to go.

Where am I going to sleep?

Which building can I break into to stay warm?

I rubbed my hands together and continued to glance around the big city.

Where do I go?

Who can help me?

I contemplated my options for a while, not sure what choice to make, but one thought stood out above the rest.

Layton?

Yes, Layton, where Dad lives.

I took my transfer slip out of my pocket and jumped on the Route 70 Bus making my way to Layton. I sat in the back corner of the bus.

How could my mother do this to me?

How could she dispose of me so easily?

The garbage bag sat on my lap. I stared out the window at the sun-spackled streets passing by and wondered what the upcoming days would bring.

That was the end of my life with Mom.

Yet, only really the beginning of my story.

the weight of it all

AFTER TWO HOURS ON the bus, I ended up in Layton, where Dad lived in the same small white house, I had left years prior. When I showed up at his house, he stared at me blankly, but invited me inside.

"Tiffany, what's going on?" he asked. "Why are you here?"

I dropped my garbage bag on the floor and took a deep breath. "Mom kicked me out."

He scratched his head and began pacing. "Why did she kick you out?"

I stared at him for a moment, then peered at the ground before looking up again. "Roger's been sexually abusing me, Dad. I told Mom what happened, and she chose him over me. She chose him." I covered my face and began to cry.

"Okay, you can stay here." He stepped into the kitchen and opened the fridge.

I couldn't tell if he was upset, angry, or if he was feeling any emotion at all. I typically could never tell how Dad was feeling because he didn't show much in the way of facial expressions. That's just how he was.

I wish I could connect to him.

"Thank you, Dad." I moved toward the couch and sat down.

Dad took me in without question, even though he could barely afford to support himself, let alone another mouth to feed. It was very different being in Dad's house without Mom. For starters, I no longer had to sleep on a tiny bed in the kitchen. Dad offered me the only bedroom in the house while he slept on the sofa bed in the living room. No one was there when I'd come home from school and there were never any rules or routines. I didn't have chores, or a bedtime, and I had much more freedom. It was a foreign transition.

Utah DCFS had a follow-up appointment with Mom about the original case against Roger trying to understand my living situation and why I had moved in with Dad. Afterwards a man came to interview me and informed me that he'd be checking in from time to time. I never shared the details with Dad about what happened with Roger, and we never discussed it. It appeared he wanted to talk about it every now and then, just didn't know how to bring it up. He'd become so introverted since the divorce that communicating with his thirteen-year-old daughter, even small talk, seemed uncomfortable, and both of us were unsure how to connect. I often wondered what feelings he harbored for Roger regarding the abuse and if he felt that he failed in his role as my protector. Yet, I didn't want to ask and make him feel that the abuse I suffered from Roger was somehow his fault.

Dad tried his best to be a good father, although it's hard for him. He had a steady job but not much money. He still had his old job as a maintenance supervisor at a hotel company, but he added a part-time janitorial job cleaning offices for a trucking company to help make ends meet. Dad had to take a bus an hour and half each way to work every day because of the fact he had lost his driver's license from the hit and run accident with grandpa's truck. He left for work at 5:00 am in the morning and usually didn't return home until around 6:00 pm. Most of his money went to Mom for child support, even though one of the kids he's paying money to support now lived with him.

There were times when there's no working phone at the house, and we use a payphone to make calls. We ate Ramen noodles or Macaroni and Cheese with hot dogs for dinner most nights. The big treat on the weekend was to have a Tony's taco pizza for dinner. I loved picking off the pepperoni's and eating them first. We did most of our grocery shopping at a place called Grocery Outlet, where they sold food that's just past its expiration date at discount prices. It wasn't easy, but I knew nothing different.

It *was* my normal.

There were times I'd sneak a peek into Dad's wallet when he'd jump in the shower. I wondered and often worried about how much money he really had. All I'd see was a $20 bill, and I knew he didn't get paid for another week or two.

How would he survive on that and pay for us to do things on the weekend?

Dad somehow always made sure that we had something to eat and to provide for us.

Even with those difficulties, living with Dad was so much better than life with Mom and Roger. I always felt loved with Dad. Whatever social or financial pressures he experienced, he left them behind when he was with me. In the time we had together, I always knew I had a movie buddy even if it was a chick flick, which 99% of the time, that's what we saw. Julia Roberts was my favorite, and he'd take me to all the movies she played in. He'd get misty-eyed at the sappy parts. When I asked if he was crying, he'd play it off that he wasn't affected by the movie, but I knew that Dad had a secret soft spot for chick flicks. Life was hard for us, but love and support cost nothing, and I was blessed to have those in abundance.

With Dad having two jobs and no car, the reality of my life was that even with his love and support, I became a classic latch key kid. Dad had to leave before I went to school in the morning, so I woke up, cooked my own breakfast, and made my way to school. After school, I walked home or went to see friends. I often ate dinner by myself, waiting for him to get back from work. It was the opposite of life with Mom. She had been like a fly that would never go away, buzzing in my ear with chaos, drama, and noise, and in my face in a invasive manner. I couldn't have a moment to myself without a million questions being asked or a task for me to do. I was on trial and a servant the moment I walked in the door. With Dad, I had the love Mom never gave me, but I'm forced to spend long swaths of time alone. I internalized a lot, trying to make sense of the things I wanted to ask my parents, but never felt that I could. Journaling and my friend, Jamie, became my space of guide and release.

I listened to music all the time. It was my constant and loyal companion. My Walkman was constantly plugged into my ears—on the way to school, between classes, and in bed at night.

Music became my solace. When it wasn't my Walkman, it was the radio. I was an avid fan, calling up requests to the local radio station and sending shout-outs to my friends. The songs pounding through my headphones took on great meaning for me. I heard my own troubles reflected in the lyrics and the energy of the music. I listened to a lot of Nine Inch Nails, Marilyn Manson, and Korn—all hard-core and dark music, which was a pretty good mirror of what I felt on the inside. I still was full of rage and confusion over Mom "throwing me away" and rocking out to the music offered an outlet for those dark currents that rushed around inside me.

While music was an outlet, it wasn't a solution. I could turn the volume up as loud as possible and it numbed things for a while, but it couldn't take away the pain that left a gaping wound in me. It started to take a toll on my life.

I had always done well at school. Even when I was bouncing around with Mom from school to school, I tried to do my best in class and get good grades. This time, though, school was different.

In Layton with Dad, I'm once again dropped into a brand-new school smack dab in the middle of a school year. However, this is junior high now. If I could survive the elementary school bouncing period, it seemed I could survive another round of getting to know new kids and teachers. After a period of relative stability for a few years on the school front, I felt as if I was back in the bouncing period. Before, when I bounced from school to school with Mom, I would always endeavor to blend in and be part of my new school community, trying to not be the spotlight in a negative way. Sometimes it worked better than other times. Yet, the very act of trying had the effect of keeping me engaged and involved in my schoolwork. Through all of my ups and downs over the years, I would always get good grades, even when I was being sexually and psychologically abused at home.

Unlike before, I couldn't find the energy or desire even to try and be part of my new school. Whatever well I drew my motivation and desire from before had run dry. The drive I once had to make the best of a situation was gone, sucked out of me by the trauma of being thrown out of my home by my own mother and forced to take a back seat to a child molester.

Instead of applying myself to my schoolwork, I spent what energy I had trying to figure out how to get out of going to school or being at school. I became very good at faking being "sick." I called Dad at work on more than one occasion, claiming that a sudden illness had come over me. He responded with concern and sent Aunt Sammi to check me out of school because of the sudden "illness." Aunt Sammi took me to get Gatorade and Chicken Noodle Soup before dropping me off at my house, where I was alone once again. I could only get away with these fake outs so many times before Dad and the school authorities got wise. Even when I was physically present, mentally I wasn't really there. I got to school in the morning, and I somehow made my way from class to class. I sat at my desk, but inside I was flat lining. I didn't pay attention like I used to, and I left school before the classes ended. I felt an incredible disconnect with classmates, and I made little effort to find new friends.

This sudden downward spiral reverberated far deeper than any of the actual abuse I had suffered. I couldn't regain my balance from the shock waves of being left behind. Mom hit me somewhere deep inside. It was like a knockout punch to my very soul, and I felt as if I was leaking the reserve and energy that had gotten me through difficult situations before. My inner flame barely flickered, and the desire to move forward seemed like too much. When I should be thinking about school and making new friends, all I could think about was Mom's choice.

She left me and threw me away.

I was garbage.

I meant nothing to her.

I tried to find things that could make me feel something other than the numbness that had taken over my body. After school, I'd grab my boombox that had two tape cassette slots and sit at the kitchen table recording music that I loved and heard off the radio. Sometimes, I'd talk to my friend, Jamie. I went to the park and swung on the swings, and occasionally, I'd shoot hoops at the basketball court there, too. On Saturdays, I'd wake up and stay in bed for hours reading a book in the Goosebump series.

But, I couldn't get past the searing truth that Mom had chosen Roger over me— her own flesh and blood daughter. Her firstborn child. I was living in a dark cave and couldn't feel anything no matter how hard I tried.

I *was* the throw-away girl.

How could she just throw me out?

Why was I being punished for being honest with her?

I told the truth. Yet, when I did speak up about the terrible things that Roger had done to me, I seemed to be the only one paying the price.

Why was Roger left to enjoy a normal life in the house with the family, while I was left to endure overwhelming confusion and dislocation?

I couldn't pretend it didn't happen or that it would get better tomorrow. I couldn't pretend that it was all just a bad dream.

The pain was raw, and it ate me every day. My own mother didn't love or want me. If my mother didn't want me, why would the world?

I fell deeper into the dark hole of depression. I quickly digress from being a straight-A student in my old school to getting C's and D's, and even a few Fs. Before, I would be horrified to bring home such a report card.

Now, I couldn't care less.

Doing well at school was the last thing on my mind. My pride and hope shattered. My teachers tried, and so did Dad, but I didn't care. All the advice and guidance went in one ear and out the other, and I took no pride in my work or appeasing my teachers. Everything felt worthless.

I felt worthless.

The days blended into one another. I was touching the bottom, and I became suicidal and anorexic getting to the lowest I'd ever been. I was giving up on my life. I didn't care about anything anymore.

How did I get to this point?

The reward for telling the truth was truly no reward.

I guess the truth *doesn't* save you.

beneath the surface

IT TOOK MOM DRIVING me into this spot of incredible darkness and loneliness to learn about the good in people and the unconditional love out there in the world. I was saved by love and kindness, a beacon of hope and a shining light, and her name was Jamie.

Jamie Schwann was my best friend from junior high school back in Salt Lake City when I lived with Mom. Even though I lived in Layton, we kept in touch as much as we could, daily if possible, although it was difficult at times because Dad's phone often got disconnected. We had a method figured out where some days, she'd call me long distance. On the days when she couldn't, I tried to gather enough quarters to call her on a payphone. I'd ride my bike to the next small town over called Kaysville. They had a local payphone tucked away at a small grocery store where I knew I wouldn't be bothered. Sometimes we'd talk for hours on end. She was one of the few friends that I kept up with, which is mostly due to her dedication. I missed her company and the fun times we used to have after school. Our relationship continued to be a bright spot in my life, a flicker of light in the gloom. But, even then the gloom didn't escape me.

I woke up one morning with an incredible sense of dread. Not the typical sense of dread that I had felt before, this time was much heavier. I thought to myself, *today's going to be the day I end my life.*

And then I had another voice in my head prompting me to listen.

If you do this, who really wins. You're letting this defeat you.

At that point, I realized I needed to get help. I viewed asking for help as a weakness, but this wasn't something I knew I couldn't ignore.

I picked up the phone and called Jamie. She asked me why I sounded more down than usual, and I told her what I was about to do.

"I don't have any desire to live. It feels as if I'm living under a cloud where everything is a blur," I said. "I can't go on another day like this."

I didn't want to be dramatic, or to concern her. I just needed to speak what was on my mind. It had *consumed* my thoughts.

How could I not talk about it especially with my best friend?

In response, Jamie paused. "Okay, this is serious. I need to talk to my parents, and I'll call you right back. Pinky promise me that you'll be there to answer the phone when I call back." *What an odd question for her to ask?*

"Okay. I promise to be here tomorrow," I said.

I felt numb inside my own protective shell, and I didn't process that she'd be deeply worried about me. I was totally clueless that she was trying to make sure I lived through the night. I agree nonetheless, and I gave her the number on the payphone I was calling from. We arranged for a time when she'd call back tomorrow.

"I promise I'll be here tomorrow," I said.

The next day, Jamie caught me off guard. "I've spoken to my parents about your situation and they'd like you to come live with us for a while, but my Dad needs to talk to your Dad first." I grip the phone, unsure what to say.

I don't want to leave my Dad.

He'll be alone.

My stomach hurt thinking about leaving my Dad alone again.

I wasn't sure how to react to this offer. It came out of the blue and I didn't know if I wanted to bounce again. Things may not have been great in Layton, but that was my home. I didn't know if I was quite ready to pack it all up and move again into the unknown. Jamie felt that my living with her family could help pull me back from the edge, and the more we chatted on the conversation, the more the move started to appeal to me. Jamie and I had always gotten along extremely well, and I knew her family and liked them very much. They cared a great deal about me; otherwise, they wouldn't have made such a generous offer. I would be returning to a school where I knew everyone and had friends. The possibility of this move didn't really feel like taking a leap into the unknown. Besides, who wouldn't want to live with their best friend?!

After some contemplation, I decided to approach Dad and see what he thought.

"Dad. Jaime and I have been talking. She mentioned to me that her parents would be happy to have me come stay with them for a while for the new school year, but her Dad would like to talk to you about if first." I stared at him with anticipation.

Dad heard me out. He peered around the room for a few minutes, seeming lost in thought.

Glancing in my general direction, he didn't make eye contact with me but paused briefly before clearing his throat. "It would be a better living situation for you." His voice wavered as he says this. "I'll talk to Brent."

It didn't take long for him to approve my decision to move in with the Schwann's.

I moved in with Jamie and her family, which consisted of her parents Brent and Charlotte, and her little sister Abbey. Their house was back in Salt Lake City, close by the high school and junior high. It's a clean and roomy rambler-style house in a nice neighborhood. I slept in Jamie's bedroom with her. I'd never lived in such a nice and orderly home. There was a basketball hoop in the driveway. The phone never got turned off, bills were paid on time, and there was always food in the fridge. I no longer wondered if I would have food for school lunch or not. It was a little bit like being back at my grandparents' home. It took some adjusting to get used to being with a new family, but not because I didn't feel welcome.

From the beginning, the Schwann's treated me as a member of the family. They created a space for me to feel completely at home. I never felt like they were looking down at me or that I was a charity case. I had the same responsibilities as the other kids. It didn't take me long to grow comfortable there, and I began to forget my troubles. I felt very safe and stationary which was a foreign state of mind to me aside from when I spent time at Grammie's. It was a great feeling and something that I craved.

For the first time in my life, this seemed as close to living a normal family life as I'd imagined. I had chores. The entire family sat down to eat meals, and we watched movies together at their home. I could almost memorize *Seven Brides and Seven Brothers* from how often we watched it. That movie was a favorite for Jamie's Dad. On the weekends, we'd go out to dinner or have barbeques together as a family. I learned how to bowl. There were set rules that were fair and clear that we all followed, and I did homework at the kitchen table right after school before I do any other extracurricular activities.

There's normalcy and consistency.

Jamie and I made our school schedules so that we had as many classes together as we could. We both had honors and enjoyed doing our homework together at night. I felt so lucky that I got to live with my best friend.

It was a whole new world.

I never really knew too much about Jamie's father, Brent. He was just another Dad. Living with him, I began to understand and appreciate him very much. He quickly became an important part of my life. Brent was the ideal man of the house. He was burly with a beard. He worked hard as a supervisor at a lumberyard to support his family, and when he came home, he spent time with us. Brent teased us constantly and was playful. I loved that! He was a kind and generous man, and also very smart. Whenever we'd encounter a big word that we didn't know, we all looked it up together in the dictionary. He liked having us learn and figure out what the words meant. Brent would say things like, "I'm a kind and benevolent father." I had no idea what benevolent meant for the longest of time. I'd never had someone make me feel smart the way he did. He inspired me and instilled in me a love of learning.

Brent had an old Dodge Ram SUV. He made a trade with Jamie and me that if we'd wash his car, he'd show us how to drive on the weekends. Jamie and I were both fifteen. We listened to NPR in the car when he drove us around. I began to call him Dad. He never asked me to, and it just came naturally as he acted more like a father than Roger ever did.

Charlotte had diabetes and had many episodes where she'd work on and off. She loved listening to the oldies' station. Whenever Jamie and I would go on shopping runs with her, she'd sing to the songs on our way there. Charlotte played Bingo once a week with her sister, and she made the most amazing potato soup.

There was no violence or fear in their house. Instead, there was support, encouragement, routine, and love. These were things that most took for granted, yet for me, it was an atmosphere that I've never experienced before. With each day that went by, I felt the ground beneath my feet stabilize a little bit more. Slowly, but surely things started to turn around for me.

Mom found where I was staying from Dad and began to call the Schwann's house begging me to come back home. "Baby. Things are better now. Come home." I asked her not to call me anymore, but she didn't listen.

Moving to the Schwann's was not the answer to all my problems, but with the support of this family, I pushed off from the bottom of the well where I had gotten stuck. I started to see the light at the end of the dark tunnel that I'd been living in for what seemed like the longest time.

With a stable family life in place, I began to really get my bearings again at school. The fog lifted. I began to care again. I regained focus on schoolwork that I had lost, and my grades went back up to straight A's. School was an area where I began to regain control. I enjoyed the positive feedback from teachers when I did well on tests, assignments, and projects. At school, this made me a bit unusual because I openly liked my teachers. The other kids enjoyed teasing me for being a "nerd" or a "teacher's pet."

I didn't care.

It didn't faze me in the least. The respect and positive feedback I got for working hard were far more important than trying to fit in and be popular. I liked the recognition I got from my teachers. Respect was important to me because it was one of the only sources of positive reinforcement I had in my life. Most kids relied on their families for unquestioned love and support. It gave them freedom and confidence, a gift that some didn't have.

It was more than I ever got from my parents. It felt good to be recognized and praised by adults. Their kind words made me feel important and special and being called "a nerd" seemed a small price to pay for that.

Good grades started to restore my self-confidence. More than that, they made me hungry to find other areas where I could prove myself to the world. Away from Mom, I now wanted to do all that I could because I felt that I was capable of being anything. I began to stretch out beyond just schoolwork and look for other places to connect and fit in.

Where else can I challenge myself?

What else can I do to prove that I belong in this world?

Out of this growing desire, I began to participate in other activities at school. I joined the orchestra and continued to play the viola, took part in the Granite Youth Symphony, participated in bowling tournaments, joined the basketball team, acted in school plays, did volunteer work, and served on the yearbook staff. I took on more and more, thriving on the challenge of it all as well as the positive results.

These experiences were teaching me the value of hard work. I loved working because I had control and being able to see and receive a tangible result. I began to realize that no one could take that away from me. I would fail at times, but with hard work hard and giving my best, no one, not Mom or anyone else, could ever take away my choices from me. No one could conquer or dominate my human spirit and drive unless I gave it to them.

I kept searching for challenges beyond schoolwork and extracurricular activities.

Somehow, I carved out enough time to get my first job. It was on the weekends at the shoe department at K-Mart. I worked as many hours as I could, and I even tried to squeeze in a few shifts during the week after school.

I loved to earn money. It was nice to have some extra cash to buy some of the little things I've never had before—make-up, clothes, something to eat at lunch other than the "free lunch" program, longer-lasting school supplies, and even a movie every now and again. The income was important to me for more reasons more than just the things it allowed me to buy. I wasn't materialistic by nature. I'd never had anything really except the bare essentials for most of my young life, and I was truly happy creating my independence. It was my money. I earned it with *my* hard work, and I wasn't dependent on anyone else. The money gave me a true feeling of control over my own life for the first time. I learned to take care of myself, and it felt empowering! But what felt even better was that Mom wasn't there to hold me down.

This was my life.

I could make choices for myself.

My desire to attempt to do everything reached an embarrassing peak when I decided to do something completely out of character and try out for the Ms. Teen Kearns Beauty Pageant.

This was by far one of the strangest things for me to do because I didn't think that people would look at me and think, "Beauty Queen."

I was lanky, all arms and legs. Gangly was a polite way to put it. However, I didn't care because I saw it as a chance to be accepted. I worked hard in rehearsals with all the other girls, and I shared the same dream with them of someone putting a crown on my head.

Why not me?

I couldn't make it to all the rehearsals due to my work schedule and balancing out school, which meant I didn't have the routine down like the other girls who could practice day in and day out, but I wanted to try anyway.

On the night of the Pageant, they had an individual talent section and a routine performance that all the contestants did together. For my talent, I chose to sing a country song called "A Broken Wing" by Martina McBride. I had practiced it for hours whenever I could, and I'd even squeeze in practice time as I'd drive to and from work, singing away. I felt confident about it.

As I got on stage to sing, my stomach twisted. I couldn't see the audience other than the first two rows because there was a huge spotlight on the stage, that blinded out the sea of people. I knew my Dad and some friends were out there somewhere and I wanted to do a good job. My hands shook, as I adjusted the mic on the stand. As the music started, I sang soft, but by the second segment, I felt my energy pick up and stood tall. I became louder in my vocals and my hands eased up on the mic. When the song ended, applause erupted.

Yes. They loved it!

I nailed my performance and sang it just like I had in all the quiet moments in my room. I was proud that I gave myself permission to shine. I walked off stage feeling like I actually had a chance at winning the competition.

When it was time to do the routine with the other contestants to Madonna's "Celebrate," I couldn't breathe. I didn't know this routine well, and this time, the spotlights hitting the stage made me feel as if I was being evaluated under a microscope. My heart picked up pace when the music turned on.

This is it.

Oh boy, here we go.

As the other contestants glided in unison around me, I stood still, not even knowing the steps. I was placed centerstage.

What's the next step?

My hands shook, and I froze, unsure what to do.

I stared at the girls around me watching the moves that they did. I tried to quickly do the same step in unison with them, but most of the routine I stomped in place and smiled.

The spotlight is shining on me in a bad way.

They can see I'm a fraud.

I'm not worthy and I suck.

Turn it off.

Place it on someone else.

I wanted to run off stage and hide, making this moment go away, but that would be even more noticeable, so I stayed and finished up the routine instead.

I was mortified.

I felt so out of place, and I bit off more than I could chew. I thought that if I had gotten Miss Teen Kearns, society would be telling me that I was beautiful. That external source of winning the beauty pageant could've been validation to all those people that told me I wasn't pretty for years, showing them how wrong they were.

I learned a lot about myself during the competition, and overall, it was a positive experience because I had stretched myself out of my comfort zone on something way foreign for me.

I was growing.

I knew I was doing a lot, but the more I did, the more I wanted to do. I was like a boulder picking up momentum down a hill.

Even with all of these positive changes beginning to take place in my life, I wasn't free yet.

I was walking home from school one day, and Mom stood outside the Schwann's house leaning against an old beat-up gold car. My shoulders stiffen and I debated walking the other way.

Mom glanced my way.

"Tiffany, sweetheart." She yelled.

I paused.

Stop yelling and drawing attention to me.

The Schwann's were still at work, and I knew that Mom wouldn't leave until she said what was on her mind. I continued to walk toward her.

"Oh baby. You need to come live with me now. Things are different and I'm no longer with Monkey boy."

Nausea hit me at the mention of the nickname mom gave the man who molested me, the same man she threw me out for.

I stood in front of her. "Who's this?"

The man with her appeared to be on drugs and when he smiled, most of his teeth were missing.

"This is Roger, my new boyfriend." She said, pointing at him.

Another Roger? What is wrong with her?

"Oh," I said, moving my hands behind my back. "How did you two meet?"

"We met at the welfare line as we were getting food stamps."

Of course, you did.

"That's nice. I'm going to go in and get some homework done." I walked away, making my way inside the house.

"You can't stay here forever. I am your mother," she yelled. "You remember that."

I didn't look back at her and stepped in through the door. Shutting the door behind me, I sat on the ground, holding my knees.

I just want her to leave me alone.

I undertook many activities to avoid dealing with the dark feelings and wounds from the abuse, forced eviction from my family home, and the emotional ties of Mom continuing to resurface. Schoolwork and extracurricular activities ensured that I never had time for those inner shadows to creep up on me. Yet, no matter how hard I worked, how well I did at school, or how kind and generous the Schwann's were, those nightmares and experiences still haunted me. They lurked just beneath the surface.

emancipation

MY UNCLE SCOTT, DAD's brother, was a mechanic and he knew I had very little money. One weekend I was visiting Dad, and an unexpected surprise was delivered to me. It was the summer before my 16th birthday. As I stepped outside, I saw a used, banana-yellow Subaru hatchback that Uncle Scott bought for me with the arrangement that I'd make payments to him. I gasped and covered my mouth, complete love at first sight. All those times taking the bus with Dad, I had envisioned one day having my own car so we didn't have to wait to get from place to place.

Holy crap. I hit the jackpot!

Finally, a car to drive! I was thrilled.

"It's a stick shift," he smirked.

I tilted my head. "I don't know how to drive a stick shift."

"Jump in and I'll take you for a spin so you can learn."

I was hesitantly excited. "Okay!" I got into the car, and I felt okay with what he showed me until we got on a hill, and he gave me an example of how the car rolls backward.

I don't like this.

My stomach gurgled.

No stomach. Not right now.

I held tight to the door handle and closed my eyes. My thoughts were going wild on how we'd roll down the hill and would crash into something down below.

I slowly opened my eyes to peek and took a deep breath as we weren't near a hill and safe on the road.

This was going to take some getting used to.

After a while, he asked if I felt confident about how to use a stick shift. I nodded and we headed back home.

Love comes in all forms, and for me, it came as a banana-yellow Subaru, which also didn't come without complications. This was my first car, and the poor Subaru had to endure some on-the-job learning from me. I burned out the clutch while learning to drive stick, and I got my first taste of bearing the brunt of car repair bills. I didn't *really* know what I was doing.

Even after I finally mastered driving a stick, I never was quite sure if the Subaru would make it all the way home or not.

Every time I took it on a long ride, I said a quiet little prayer to myself that we'd make it.

The Subaru was neither the most fashionable nor most reliable of cars. I nickname it "my jitney" or "banana boat."

At the beginning of junior year, I drove it to school, and the other kids with their new cars would make fun of me. Sometimes, it even broke down right in front of the school, and I needed to get out and push it.

I didn't care.

That little Subaru wasn't exactly pretty or slick, but it was *all* mine, and I loved it. I enjoyed picking up Trent and Trina after school to go and do things together. The Subaru was a godsend and made a huge difference in getting me to school every day, a challenge I had faced previously. It also became a godsend in being a resource that allowed me to provide security for me and my siblings.

My car became a safe haven and a little home for me. I added extra special touches that gave it the energy and joy that I couldn't find anywhere else. I put in an old home speaker system that I found at the thrift store. It took up the whole backseat. When you turned it on, the amp vibrated my car and the mirrors beat to the rhythm of the music, creating waves of high energy that felt as if I was having a dance party. I loved it! I decorated my car with air fresheners to invite a sense of home into my space, and I handwashed it multiple times a month. I loved and took great care of my "banana boat" and it supported me in many ways not seen or understood by anyone but me.

It didn't have an air conditioning, so on hot days I'd roll down the windows trying not to sweat to death. Most of the time, I'd still show up to work with a sweat stain on my back and my hair all disheveled. But, it was mine and I loved it!

I liked to take my siblings on car rides where I would ram into dumpsters with my car to make them laugh. My car had a thick rubber bumper, so I always thought that made it extra protected. I'd go into a parking lot and spin around in circles.

"Watch my car. Watch what I can do," I'd say.

Trina, my sister, laughed hysterically, so I'd continue to do it.

Mom still attempted to have me come back home to live with her. She reminded me that she was getting better, but every time I had encounters with her, I didn't know if I could trust what she was saying this time. One day, I caught wind that Mom, in her lackadaisical parenting ways, sent Trina and Troy to school in summer clothes on a day with a massive snowstorm.

What was she thinking?

Was she intoxicated this morning and not aware of them?

I knew they would be walking home from school, and I raced toward their elementary to try and find them.

Please, let me find them.

I clung to the steering wheel, feeling the urge to strangle mom for not thinking about their needs. I found them quickly on their normal route that they walked and pulled over to let them into the car. I was so grateful to be able to pick them up from school without coats and provide them a safe and warm space in my car. When I dropped them off, Mom laid on her bed, just like she normally did.

"How could you not have them take their coats to school. It's freezing outside." Mom continued watching her show without saying a word to me.

"What's wrong with you?" I screamed.

She ignored me and carried on with her beloved soap.

I left enraged that she could even call herself a mother. She still showed me the same things she's been showing me for years—she couldn't be trusted, and she would never change.

A notice of cancelation for my car insurance came in the mail. I called my agent and asked why my insurance was being canceled.

"Your mom called and said you didn't need it anymore." *Why would she do that?*

"What? That's not true," I yelled. "Why would I not need it anymore?"

He paused.

He didn't know the dynamics between mom and I, and it wasn't his fault that this happened. I knew that. I wanted to yell at someone, but he wasn't the one to do that to.

"I'm sorry," I said. "I still need my insurance."

"Absolutely. We'll get that all sorted out." *She always tries to take my joy.*

Sitting in class, I tried to focus on what was being taught while my mind worried about the upcoming year as a Junior. The intercom came on and I tilted my head to listen to what the announcement was. Knowing what was going on helped me to feel more grounded even if it had nothing to do with me.

"Tiffany Barnes, please come down to the main office." I stared at the intercom.

Did they say my name? Why?

Kids in the class turned around and peered at me as if to say, "that's you."

I leaned back in my chair and felt the urge to hide and pretend like I didn't hear my name being called, even though I did. Grabbing my backpack, I slowly stood and made my way out of class with all eyes on me. I could feel them. This wasn't how I liked to be seen.

I made my way to the main office and saw a nicely dressed man with brown hair, about 5'10 standing by the check-in area. It took me a moment to realize that it was the state social worker who had visited me previously.

My stomach gurgled and I began to feel sick. Stepping into the office, the receptionist took a sip from her mug and gave me a wide grin. "This gentleman would like to chat with you." I peered at him. "Hi Tiffany. It's good to see you again. I have a few questions to ask you. Would that be okay?"

Standing still, my stomach cramped, and I nodded.

Here comes that pain again.

I followed him outside the main office where he took a seat on a bench, and I sat next to him, holding my hand.

"I'm just doing a follow-up with you. Your mom reported you as a run-away, and the state just wants to understand what's going on." *A run-away? Why would she say that?*

I didn't understand and I looked at the ground. My legs shook with the mention of "Mom", and rage bunched through my hands.

She threw me away. She gets child support. Why can't she just leave me alone?

"Are you a runaway, Tiffany?" he asked.

I shook my head. "No. My mom told me to leave, and my Dad gave me permission to live with a family friend."

He pulled a notebook out of his briefcase and grabbed a pen. "The Schwanns?"

"Yes. That's right." I said.

Clearing his throat, he gazed at me. "We've talked with your Dad and the Schwanns. Your story checks out, but legally, you need to either go with your Mom or Dad, unless you consider emancipation.

Emancipation?

I don't want to go with Mom or Dad.

I have to leave the Schwanns?

I wanted to stay with Jamie and her family. I loved being able share a room with my best friend and have classes with her. I didn't want to change the consistency that I had grown accustomed to. It was ideal for me. Why now, is Mom taking this from me?

I don't want to just walk away from them and seem ungrateful for what they've done.

Will they understand that?

"What is that?" I asked. "Emancipation?"

He told me that emancipation was the process set up by the state of Utah to separate an individual from their parents legally. The state granted emancipation when they believed that the applicant had proven that they were able to support and take care of themselves independently of their legal guardians. "I've got to be honest with you though the odds are stacked against you. There's only one other case in the state of Utah that's ever been granted emancipation at your age," he said.

Well, haven't the odds already been stacked against me? Why don't I go for it? Worst case scenario, the judge says no. Why not take the next step and have the law recognize what's already the truth?

I hesitated.

I don't want to leave my best friend.

Living with Jaime was like a party every day. My stomach tightened, unsure if I wanted to go through with it. Part of me didn't want to formalize the reality of being all on my own. It was the same part of me that wished that somehow things were different and that my life could be like other kids, living safely and comfortably under the same roof as their parents.

But, the Schwanns had given me a place and had become a refuge for me. They had created a family environment filled with love, consistency, and memories.

Good memories.

I had wanted this for so long and leaving felt like a giant slap in the face to them for all that they had done. I told him that I would think about it and get back to him. He gave me his card before he left and promised to check in.

The more the idea of emancipation sat with me, the more appealing it became. I knew in my gut that the social worker was right. I already wasn't attached to my parents in any real way.

I'd come this far, and I wasn't going to go back. The force driving me to move forward with emancipation was an intense desire to be truly free of Mom. I understood that she would never be in any shape or condition to be the mother that I wished and longed for. My practical side sets in, and I want more than anything to make sure that she doesn't have the capacity to disrupt the life I was slowly building for myself.

Without emancipation, I was aware that mom could continue to treat me as a runaway, and to have control over my life. It wasn't just me that I was worried about. I was concerned that Mom would somehow come after the Schwann's for taking me in. The last thing I would ever want was for them to somehow get in trouble for their good deed. I knew what Mom was capable of. I no longer wanted to live with that fear hanging over me. Realizing all this, I decided to face whatever challenges emancipation would present in order to be free of the woman who caused so much trouble and pain in my life.

I called the state social worker to let him know what I had decided.

The concept of emancipation was strange to me at first. I thought it would be an epic legal event with hearings and detailed interviews, but it wasn't. Like most government actions, it was mostly an exercise in filling out endless forms. I went and picked up the forms at the state courthouse. I filled them out, and I was shocked at how simple the emancipation process seemed.

The hardest part of the process, and the one part that I couldn't do on my own was I had to get both my parents to sign the final notarized form. I knew Dad would understand that this was the best thing for me.

I knew Mom would be a different story. I called Mom and I told her that I wanted to come over.

"Oh baby, I knew you'd come around," she said.

I gathered my courage to go see her and knocked on the door. The door opened immediately, and a younger kid answered the door and stared up at me.

Who's this kid?

I walked in and was immediately taken back by the foul odors of mold and cigarettes. The walls held fish nets and pictures of Marlin, and there were fish tanks all over the living room. I stared in disbelief at the junk piled all over the floor, something that Mom never would've allowed before with the *other* Roger.

Where is Mom?

Where is Trina, Trent, and Troy? Why didn't they come to the door?

My heart picked up pace as I walked toward sound coming from inside her bedroom.

The TV. Of course.

I wasn't surprised when I found her sitting on the bed watching her new soap, smoking away with a bag of Doritos at arm's reach. Her new man was there too, neither of them giving a care about anything happening around them.

Things never change.

She stared at me as if she was confused on why I was there, even though we just talked on the phone about me coming over.

I stepped in place uncertain what to do. "Where are the kids?"

Mom pointed out her door, but still had her eyes fixated on the TV, stuffing her face with handfuls of chips.

"Where are they? I asked.

She cleared her throat and kept her eyes locked on the TV. "They're out back playing on the trampoline."

I stared in the general direction of where they'd be.

Maybe I should stay, and I could make it better for them?

"I need you to sign these," I said, handing her the emancipation papers. "I know you want me to come live with you, but I don't think this is a good situation. I have a job and I'm already supporting myself."

She sat up and sneered at me. "What are they?"

I cleared my throat. Calmly, I explained to her the emancipation process and that I needed her to sign the form for me. Placing the documents on her bed, I held my ground.

"What about the child support?" she asked. She folded her arms like she was about to throw a fit.

Oh, shit! I didn't think about that.

I ground my teeth.

"I don't know why you don't love me," she said. "I know I made some mistakes, but I don't know why you don't give me a chance."

Why? You didn't give a fuck about me when you were with Roger. Let me go.

"Why did you report me as a run-away when you kicked me out?" I asked.

Mom lit a new cigarette and a took a few puffs, blowing smoke in the air, and pointed it nonchalantly at me. "I'm not signing those."

I snatched the documents from her bed. "The states going to believe me anyway. You have a file longer than two filing cabinets." I stomped out of her room. "You don't care about anyone but yourself."

Before I left, I went to the backyard and ran to give my siblings a hug. They were dirty and unkept, just like I had been at their age, when I was constantly bullied in school. I held them tight and jumped on an old trampoline with them. It had a few missing springs, and I hoped that it would hold up. They were happy to see me, and I was ecstatic to see them.

Maybe I could stay until I'm eighteen?

The other part of me resisted as I already had freedom and I wasn't going to be tied down again.

I said goodbye and tried to swallow down the emotion bunching in my throat—remorse.

I went back a few more times, trying to convince her, but she wasn't interested. I begged Dad for his help in trying to make it happen.

"I'm willing to still pay her," he said.

I stood tall and my eyes grew wide. "Really? That would be awesome, Dad."

He nodded. "I'll take care of it," he responded in a low voice.

My father, as is his way, was willing to make incredible personal sacrifices in order to help me. Eventually, he bribed Mom to sign the emancipation forms by agreeing to continue providing her with the full child support payments, just like he told me he would. Mom had no hesitations to that arrangement with him, and she signed the forms.

I handed the now-notarized emancipation forms into the state. There was a perfunctory appearance before a judge, but not much else.

Then, I waited.

Freedom was on the horizon.

bittersweet

IN MY JUNIOR YEAR, Ms. Riddley was my Child Development teacher, and it was her first-year teaching. She was teacher advisor for our school's chapter of the Family, Career, and Community Leaders of America, also known as FCCLA. Ms. Riddley always was put together and well dressed. She was in her early twenties, making her more relatable than other teachers I've had. Ms. Riddley cared deeply about her students, and unlike many teachers, she wanted to hear about her students' lives. This wasn't the usual practice for teachers, who quickly learn where to draw the line to not be overwhelmed by getting involved with their students' home lives.

Near the second half of the school year, suddenly, Ms. Riddley took a leave of absence.   I was very concerned about her well-being at that time. She was a safety net for me.

What if she doesn't come back?

What felt like forever to me, was only a couple of weeks for her. I was overjoyed when Ms. Riddley came back to school.

One morning I came to school early to turn in an assignment to Ms. Riddley. When I turned in the papers, I stumbled into the FCCLA meeting she was leading. There were a bunch of girls eating bagels, laughing, and having a good time. I apologized for interrupting and started to leave, but Ms. Riddley invited me to stay.

She wants me to stay?

I smiled and took a seat at one of the tables. That was the beginning of my involvement with FCCLA.

They asked me to join, and I was happy to be part of it all. Once again, it felt luminous to be part of a team, but more importantly, this was the start of my relationship with Ms. Riddley.

I struggled with an eating disorder and was anorexic.

Even after my time with the Schwann's and my growing self-confidence, I still had terribly low self-esteem. Mom had always told me from the earliest day I could remember that I was ugly and fat, and part of me couldn't shake that. Growing up constantly hearing that I wasn't good enough, I was ugly, and that mom should've aborted me, became more than just words and eventually, I started to believe them.

One day after school, Ms. Riddley and I walked out to the school parking lot as we are both about to head home for the day. While walking, she gently asked me questions about my life. At first, I was hesitant to talk to her about it. I felt embarrassed and ashamed. I wanted to just leave things in my past and not think about them, but she had a sweet, loving manner where I couldn't help but answer her.

Once I started sharing my life with her, the floodgates opened. Ms. Riddley stood in the parking lot for hours with me as I told her everything about Mom trying to come back into my life after throwing me out, my abusive family situations and the molestation, living alone, and my eating disorder. I'd never had someone really listen to me like this. Telling someone the darkest parts of my soul and having them care and be present was foreign to me. She stayed with me long after school was over, all the way into the evening.

"You're amazing and a beautiful young woman."

I looked at her for a moment, taking in what she said to me. I could see a genuine care within her eyes, and that felt good, but also uncertain. My trust issues were always close on the surface. I peered at the ground.

"Say, thank you," she said. "It's good to receive what other's see in you."

I squirmed in discomfort and nodded.

"Okay, thank you," I said softly, staring at the ground.

"I have an idea," she said. "You should write down everything that you eat and we can go over it together."

I don't understand. To me healthy is thin, and thin is beautiful. I feel good and comfortable like this.

Why do I need to track my food?

"What's the purpose of doing that?" I asked, folding my arms.

She lightly smiled and touched my arm. "You're pretty thin, Tiffany."

"Yes, I know. Isn't that great?"

"Not like this. You're unhealthy thin," she said. "The food journal will help us to see that you're getting the nutrition that your body needs. I'll bring you some of my cookbooks that you can take a look at."

I look down at the ground. "Okay."

She rubbed my shoulder and gently encouraged me to read the nutrition books because they had "good content," as she put it. She wanted to know more about my home life and the underlying struggles causing my eating issues. I listened to her advice, and I felt valued, seen, and heard.

That conversation was the beginning of a long relationship. One day after school, I picked up Troy and Trina and brought them to meet Ms. Riddley. She loved Troy's red hair! We sat and chatted about my thoughts on the emancipation process, and she gave her presence to me and my siblings. I enjoyed being around Ms. Riddley, as she was a great listener to me, but she also was uplifting and a huge cheerleader of mine. She encouraged me to not hide, and to face my feelings. She told me often that I was beautiful, talented, and smart, and expressed to me constantly that I was full of potential. For the first time, I believed it. I felt like a radiant light and gift around her.

She bought me a journal and encouraged me to write in it. It had been a while since I had written in a journal, and it felt as if I was coming back to dear friend who patiently waited for me to visit with them again. She inscribed the journal, and her inspiring message of hope and love meant the world to me. I often came back and read what she wrote. It was a meaningful gift more valuable than she may have realized. She gave me motivational tapes from John Bytheway that helped with my self-esteem. No one had ever taken such a deep interest in me or tried to actively help me like this.

I took Ms. Riddley's advice and read some of the nutrition books she gave me and started making changes in my lifestyle. I ate three meals a day, including breakfast, unlike my once-a day meal routine that I had been doing. The internal dialogue about my weight and how thin meant being beautiful and enough, still haunted me. But what carried me through was I really wanted Ms. Riddley to praise me, and I thrived off the accountability check-ins with her. I valued her opinion, and I didn't want to let her down. She was the person that gave me the strength and support I needed to truly forge a path out of the darkness of the abuse I had suffered under Mom.

Each year the FCCLA had a statewide convention. Part of that convention was a competition where students from across the state made presentations on their chosen subjects.

With Ms. Riddley's encouragement, I decided to enter the competition. As my entry, I chose to do a talk on child abuse. It was the first time I'd really looked into the subject from another angle other than my own. I did the research, and I was amazed and shocked to find out how widespread abuse *truly* was. The statistics were sobering.

One in four girls, and one in six boys experienced some form of abuse *before* the age of eighteen. The stats said it was more likely a child would be abused before the age of eighteen than it was that they would play a high school sport or go to college. It hit me like a ton of bricks. The numbers were impossible to ignore.

Abuse *was* an epidemic.

I was disgusted and sick to my stomach reading that, and I was deeply impacted, realizing abuse wasn't just happening to me. I felt understood and seen. I wasn't such an anomaly which I had felt for many years.

I worked with Ms. Riddley on my FCCLA presentation. She helped me prepare poster boards outlining my subject. I rehearsed in front of her after school, and I learned to weave my story together with the larger issues of child abuse in this country. She complimented my research and progress, and she constantly cheered me on.

Finally, the big day arrived. I traveled to the statewide FCCLA convention and presented what I had worked on to the judges. I sat in the hallway waiting for my turn to present, and paid attention to others around me that were practicing their presentations.

I don't stand a chance.

I watched as they held up their professionally organized posters, in their nice clothes, that I couldn't afford.

Wow. These people are way more prepared and cuter than me.

I frowned and my stomach gurgled and cramped in reply to my inner thoughts.

Here we go again.

I really got tired of the discomfort pain I felt in my stomach whenever I grew nervous or worried. I wondered if others were examining and judging me for what I was wearing.

I should leave.

No. What will your FCCLA group think? What would Ms. Riddley think if I don't even try?

My name was called, and I stood, grabbing my poster. I took a deep breath and put my head down as I walked inside where three judges sat at a table on the opposite side of the room.

"Hello. You're Tiffany Barnes?" a judge asked.

I glanced up and nodded, confirming her question.

"Wonderful. You can use this table for your poster board if you'd like," she said, pointing in the direction of a table at the front of the room. "Go ahead and start your presentation when you're ready."

I smiled nervously and displayed my posterboard on the table and began sharing the presentation that I had been working on with Ms. Riddley.

They sat silently, taking notes as I spoke.

"What are they writing?"

I continued with my presentation and moved beyond the statistics, telling these strangers my story about my own abuse. Their faces held awestruck and softened as I spoke to the depth of my life. I paused.

They smiled at me, and I felt a second wind to keep going with what I was saying. It was the first time I had shared at this level to anyone.

It was scary at first because I had never given a presentation before. I had been used to being in front of people performing and being judged, as I had done my viola federations up at the University of Utah for a few years, but this was completely out of my comfort zone. I was taking the negative experiences I had endured and changing the cycle to create positive ones.

I'm not alone in this.

I am exactly the right person to be sharing this.

I smiled back at the judges subconsciously realizing those truths. I wasn't the only one that had this happen to them. It was a powerful realization, and it allowed me to step out of the solitary cave that I'd been living in all these years. Being abused was NOT my fault. It was an *epidemic* that happens to more children than we'd like to imagine. There were others out there just like me who had survived and prospered.

Their stories could help me, and my story could help them.

The truth set me free.

In between breakout classes at the conference, I sat at a banquet table with Ms. Riddley and got a "Tiffany Epiphany."

My eyes grew feeling into this idea and I bounced on my chair as fire ignited within me.

"I got an idea! I should start a club for kids just like me that are going through abuse. What should I call it?"

Ms. Riddley leaned in with excitement. "I don't know. What would you call your club?'

"What about The Resilient Kids?" I asked, hesitantly.

"That could work. How does that feel to you?"

My shoulders sank. It didn't feel right. "No, it needs something more."

I grabbed the notepad I was given at the conference center and began writing words that sparked empowerment to me.

"Kids Ignited Against Abuse?" No.

"Latchkey Kids?"

Students Empower Against Abuse?

I paused and stared at what I wrote on my paper. "What about S.H.A.R.E?"

"What does it stand for?" she asked.

I shrugged. "I'm not sure." I wrote different acronyms down on a piece of paper trying to

figure out what sounded best.

No. Not that one.

Helping the Abused?

Helping the Abused!

I like that.

I played with options scribbling away as my brain sparked excitement for this beautiful idea that felt so right. I could see in my mind when we would meet, how it would be, and the impact and feeling this group would have on students.

Students React and Empower.

That's it!

Putting my pen down on the table, I raised my hands in the air. "I got it," I yelled. Noise rustled behind me, and I gazed back to see that I had an audience. I slowly turned in my chair toward Ms. Riddley, still smiling from ear to ear even though I had eyes on me.

Ms. Riddley stared at me with anticipation. "Tell me."

"Students Helping the Abused React and Empower!" I said, smiling from ear to ear.

She reached for my hand and patted the top of it. "I love it. That's a fantastic idea!"

Later on that evening, the judges awarded me the highest marking, and I received the gold medal at the competition.

"I'm so proud of you, Tiffany." Ms. Riddley was beaming.

I loved recognition, words of affirmation, and being seen. It was extremely rewarding receiving all these things that had seemed so rare to me. Getting the gold medal for my repetition and hard work, and not leaving empty handed made me feel like I was happily floating.

The joy of the reward was only tempered when Ms. Riddley told our FCCLA group at a meeting that she was transferring to another school the upcoming year and she wouldn't be our FCCLA advisor anymore. I was going to be the president of the chapter the following year. I wanted her to be there with me for my senior year as I graduated and got my diploma. I looked down at the ground and got really quiet.

Why would she leave?

Why doesn't she want to stay with us?

I could transfer to the school where she's going to.

I held my hands together and gazed around the room.

This isn't real.

There goes another person leaving me.

I couldn't transfer schools again just when I was grounded and rooted, and she couldn't stay. There was only a month until school got out and that didn't offer much time to cherish what moments I had left with her.

I felt heartbroken. I got so close to her that I was devasted. It brought me back to my abandonment issues of people always seeming to leave. After that, I didn't want to see her after class anymore. I couldn't get even closer and felt my heart shatter more. I felt resentment about not understanding why Ms. Riddley couldn't wait a year until I had graduated school, before she decided to pack things up.

I kept my distance with everyone. I had internalized a lot about it and cried often as the hope of next year and all the grandiose possibilities had vanished on the day that she said, "I'm leaving."

I began ditching school, working more and not involving myself in things. I had closed myself off again.

When the year came to an end, I walked slowly into Ms. Riddley's room and asked her to sign my yearbook.

This is the last time I'm going to see her.

She smiled at me. "Of course, I will."

I gave her my yearbook, and she took time writing me a heartfelt message within my book. She let me know that her number was on the page and that she'd love to stay in contact with me. I wanted to read the message, but I didn't want her to see me cry so I thanked her and left the room instead.

Once I got home, I sat on my bed and read the message that Ms. Riddley wrote in my book.

"Tiffany, you have taught me so much this year. You're amazing. Say (thank you). Good luck with everything. I know you'll succeed in whatever you decide to do. Keep in touch and remember I love ya."

I closed the book and hugged it, holding her message closer to my heart as tears dripped down my cheeks.

I'm not ready to say goodbye.

I couldn't express myself well, but music was one way that I tried to communicate with others when I didn't know how to covey how I felt. I spent time trying to find just the right songs as they were the spokesperson to my soul. I made cd's often for my friends to connect with them. Near the end of the school year, I pulled in the parking lot right next to Ms. Riddley's car. I put a note on her window letting her know how sad I was that she was leaving, and I printed out the lyrics of a song that reminded me of her, Sarah Mclachlan, "I Will Remember You."

Knowing that I still had a way of contacting Ms. Riddley so she wasn't completely gone and having my yearbook with her message, held me in the moments when I didn't feel hopeful about life.

More than my schoolwork or extra-curricular, my relationship with Ms. Riddley impacted me in a way that was a giant new step for me. Winning the gold medal was the climax of our time together. I'd taken a big step forward and found a way to confront the storm that had been with me ever since being thrown out by Mom. Turning a negative experience into a positive one allowed me to be a happier and freer person. For me, that reason was to be an example of overcoming abuse and empowering others to do the same.

It had been incredible how far a little belief went. Ms. Riddley didn't do anything superhuman, she just took the time to care and believe in me.

I was in a stable home with Dad's blessing. I'd found solace and reward in hard work, both in school and in the working world, and I no longer struggled with anorexia as much as I did at the beginning of the year.

You're amazing Tiffany. I'm so proud of you. I could hear her say in my mind.

The social worker visited me at school. He was excited and pulled me out of class to share the news that the state had signed off on the emancipation. He gave me the final forms authorizing the transfer of guardianship.

"It's official," he said.

Standing there in the high school hallway, I stared at him and then looked down at the forms in a mild state of shock.

I can't believe Mom really went through with it.

I felt like fireworks were going off within me, sparking both joy and freedom. I could breathe.

I was now legally my own guardian.

I have to tell Ms. Riddley!

Once the state social worker left, my feet picked up pace and I ran to Ms. Riddley's room, smiling the whole way. I opened her door to tell her, except she's not there. A new teacher sat in the chair Ms. Riddley used to occupy.

Oh, that's right. She's at a different school now.

She's left.

I was reminded of her absence. I stared at the ground and dropped my hands to my side, closing the door.

In the darkest moments when the demons inside me tried to come out, I could hear Ms. Riddley's encouraging and affirming words in my mind, bringing me back to the light.

"I'm so proud of you" I could hear her say. I will miss her. I was hopeful of what senior year would bring.

My experiences in life won't hold me down. I refused to use it as a crutch. Instead, I wanted to use it as a stepping-stone to a brighter future.

I was in charge of my own life.

I was ready to take the next step to be truly free.

CHAPTER EIGHTEEN

freedom

THE EMANCIPATION PROCESS SET off other changes
besides just legally freeing myself from Mom. I've been very
happy living with the Schwann's. They gave me so much
and taught me about the meaning of family. Yet, there was
something deep inside gnawing at me.

Even amidst the love and stability in Jamie's family, I felt a
sense of rootlessness. The independence I discovered through
schoolwork, a paying job, and legal emancipation had fortified
my desire to not ask anyone for *anything* again. I loved the
Schwann's, but I didn't want them to feel like they had to take
care of me. I'd rather take care of it myself.

Make my own way.

Soon after the emancipation was completed, I told Jamie
and her parents that I wanted to move out and get my own
place. They told me that I was always welcome there, but they
respected my decision.

I packed up my things from the room I shared with Jamie and paused as I looked around taking in the memories and joy of the time I spent here. My heart ached as I walked out of the bedroom and made my way up to the front room where the Schwann's family awaited me. I put my box down and gave each one of them a hug. As I got to Mrs. Schwann, she held me tightly.

"I've so enjoyed having you here, and I'm going to miss you."

I was taken back by her embrace and comment as she'd never vocally expressed this to me before. I didn't know she cared this much about me. I sunk into her hug for a while longer.

"I'm going to miss you too," I said, before letting go and walking out of the Schwanns home.

I took on a second job to help bolster my case that I could be a responsible person who supported myself. I worked as a waitress at Frontier Pies. This was where I reconnected with an old friend of mine from elementary school named Krista. It was her dad that mom used to perform sexual favors on in exchange for recording time for her music when we live in the blue house. She was in the same high school with me, but we weren't really close until we're brought back together working at Frontier Pies. Krista was a little older than me and had an older sister who'd moved out of the family home when she was a teenager. She wanted to do the same thing as her sister, to get away from her demanding LDS parents. I told her of my plan to strike out on my own, and she suggested that we do it together. I agreed, thrilled to have a partner in this next step in my life.

I thought that we were on top of the world, living with no parents, and tackling the world together, and imagined it was going to be this grandiose thing. Krista and I rented a basement apartment for five hundred dollars. Our landlords were a newlywed couple who'd just graduated from medical school. They were a little nervous about having two teenage girls as tenants, and I had to show them my emancipation papers before they were willing to offer us a lease. It was the first, but not the last time, I used the emancipation papers to put people at ease about my unusual situation.

When I went shopping for furniture for our new apartment, I showed my papers to the store owner, and he kindly gave me credit to buy a futon and bed frame. I felt such a huge relief because my biggest concern was figuring out how I would pay for everything when I had a rent check due at the end of each month.

My name was on the lease, and I constantly worried that either I would come up short or Krista wouldn't deliver her half of the rent. Living on my own was exciting, but it also was a huge change of pace from living with my parents or the Schwann's. I felt a lot more pressure and anxiety to perform perfectly, responsibly, and to never take my eye off my target. Depression still sat with me, and I no longer had Ms. Riddley to lift me up.

At school, I never broadcasted my unique situation, but whenever the other kids found out I lived on my own, they thought it was cool. "Wow, you're so lucky! You can do whatever you want," they say. Or I'd be bullied because of my "special circumstance."

When they thought of me, they thought it was just a party all the time. For the most part, the kids thought that it sounded great because I could legally check myself in and out of school whenever I wanted. I became resentful of them for getting cars from their parents, going home to a fridge full of food, and never needing to worry about pinching pennies to make it by. They had no idea just how good they had it. Just trying to push myself to get to school, took more effort, like walking through quicksand.

One day, I was late for my third-period class. As I walked into the room, I wrote myself an excuse note.

"Please excuse Tiffany Barnes for being late. Thank you."
Tiffany Barnes

I handed it to Mrs. Linares, and some kid on the front row said, "Well, that's not fair. We don't get to write our own excuse notes. How come she gets to?"

I glanced at him with annoyance and took my seat. When the bell rang to end third period, some kids followed me out of the room, inquiring about my situation. I let them know that I was emancipated. They didn't know what that entailed, so I told them what it meant and why I was my own guardian. One of the kids confidentially expressed to me that they were going through something similar at home.

A lightbulb went off, and I had another "Tiffany Epiphany." It was as if a voice in my head said, "This is why you didn't take your life. You're meant to be a catalyst for others to speak up and speak loud against abuse."

I should start the support group I thought about last year, for kids like me who are going through abuse or have gone through it. In that moment, a foot stepped from the quicksand I had been in. I smiled, feeling my purpose. The thought fed my flame, giving me hope and something to strive for. When I helped others, it internally healed me as well. I immediately started a support group called S.H.A.R.E. There were ten of us in the group, and there wasn't a formality to it. We helped each other in multiple ways. We were a shoulder to cry, a listening ear, an anchor for each other to stay on a healthy path away from drugs, teen pregnancy, and other toxic behaviors that were easy to fall into without support. If we had classes together, we'd do homework with each other. It was a safe space. I still had some work to do to get my other foot off the ground, but this was a start, a different beginning.

After hearing about our support group, a teacher reached out to me and expressed her desire to have me come speak to her class about recognizing the signs of abuse. That set off a chain reaction where I began reaching out to other schools and teachers to also speak to their class.

During UEA break, I was invited to speak to a school's administrators and principals called "The Principals Academy," located in Provo. I talked about recognizing the signs of abuse that a child may be displaying at their school.

The teachers and staff at school were a little more understanding of my situation. For the most part, they treated me exactly like any other student. Yet, there were moments when they did what they could to help. The choir and basketball teams didn't ask me to pay the entire team dues because they knew I couldn't. During Christmas time, some of the teachers pitched in and bought me a small Christmas tree and a few presents, as well. I was both totally surprised and moved by the gesture. Guilt also clung to me as I couldn't shake the feeling that I was a charity case. The truth of emancipation and living on my own— it was hard. While all the other kids went home at night to their families where dinner was waiting on the table, I had bills to pay, clothes to buy, and homework to do. I thought that because I chose to be emancipated, that I also chose to be on my own and I shouldn't ask for help. Depression wasn't friendly during that time.

It wasn't easy, nor did it come cheap. There were so many expectations with holidays, and when I was barely scraping by, it was better to not make a huge deal out of it. There was always a longing for a family member to take the initiative to want to be with me. I missed Grammie remembering me as her dementia took over, and no one else reached out. That void felt heavy.

There were times I couldn't make rent and tried to sneak into the house just to get by for another few days. Because of this, I took a third job on the weekends working at the Bed, Bath and Beyond. I enrolled in the work release program at school that allowed me to leave early and get school credits for the time I worked. I had a job at Shopko from 12:00- 4:00 pm, had a break to eat and do homework from 4:00-5:00 pm, and then I went straight to Frontier Pies which was right next to Shopko. I started waitressing at Frontier Pies at 5:00 pm and didn't finish up usually until 11:00 pm.

They were long hours, but the Frontier Pies job offered up some important benefits. I could eat my dinner at the restaurant, so I didn't need to figure out how to feed myself that night, and I left my waitress shifts with cash in my pocket from tips. I used that money to pay for groceries or bus fare to get home when my little my "banana boat" would break down. Being on my feet all day was hard and people were not considerate about their messes and cleaning up after themselves, but the job was a lifesaver.

It kept me afloat.

Even with the three jobs, money was tight paying for food, school fees, rent, and gas. I made payments on my cap and gown, graduation announcements, and I also put down money for a class ring. I didn't own a phone. Instead, I used the payphone at the nearby McDonald's to make calls. Even then, I only had enough change to place the call.

I asked people to call me back on the payphone. It was embarrassing. Besides the meals, I got at Frontier Pies, food wasn't abundant. I'd get cans of food and Ramen at the case lot sales, and often times kidney beans and saltine crackers were what I ate. Sometimes, I'd open the cupboards thinking I'd find something different in there to eat that Krista might have contributed and brought home to share, but it was always the same items—the ones I bought and paid for. One perk for me was that Ramen noodles and canned foods were an easy clean-up and less dishes, which I appreciated without having a dishwasher.

Living on my own wasn't nearly as glamorous as the kids at school or I had made it out in our heads. Even while living on my own and working three jobs, I was still trying to push myself in school. I didn't see my new situation as an excuse to take it easy in school. I was enrolled in all honor classes, on the girls' basketball team, first chair viola in the regional youth orchestra and school orchestra, President of our school's FCCLA chapter, a member of the Spanish club and Yearbook staff, and a member of the concert choir.

Jamie and I had a falling out and we went from being best friends, to not seeing or talking to each other much. Being busy helped me not to think about how much that hurt, but I missed my best friend, and longed to have her back in my life like it once used to be.

With the three jobs, it was hard to come home and do my homework. After my shifts, I was always dead tired. Cracking open my homework was the *last* thing I wanted to do, but after being emancipated, I put on this armor that I had to be responsible and that there was no time for play.

Krista, my roommate, was opposite my personality and she wasn't very helpful. She thought that moving out was like a party every day and lived life in the moment as a free spirit. Unlike me, she didn't value her schoolwork. She was more interested in *boys*. While I burned the midnight oil finishing my homework, I tried not to pay attention to the sounds of love coming from Krista's bedroom. I wanted to be like her, more playful and have fun, but my ego and my protective shield didn't agree with those choices. The survival part within me told me that this was the only way to live and to make it out okay. I had to look out for myself, and I felt resentment that I couldn't "let go" in my life.

I didn't go to bed until past midnight most nights. I lived by the University of Utah, on the other side of town from my high school. When my car wasn't working, I had to get up at 4:00 am to take that two-hour long bus ride across town to get to school on time. It was hard, sometimes *really* hard. There were days that I would rather not go to school, especially in the winter when it was still dark and cold outside when I got up. It would be so much easier to stay in my warm bed, where there weren't parents around to force me to go. I could do whatever I wanted.

I was emancipated. Yet, something deep inside got me up on the cold mornings. I knew if I took one day off, it would be that much easier to take the next day off.

I got out of bed.

Car or no car, I tried to make it to school.

I made lists and filled up my school planner to avoid losing track of all the moving pieces going on. I loved to be organized, and I felt in control when I was. I didn't realize how much my depression had taken over, until my Dad called.

"Hey. The school called and informed me that you've been missing a bunch of days at school."

I held the phone tight.

Why do you even care? I'm emancipated.

You dropped out of high school.

I didn't say anything to him.

I was struggling. I didn't reach out to anyone, and I was feeling like a failure internally, but I was scared to let someone in. I'm embarrassed and disappointed with myself that my dad had to tell me that I was behind.

I thought I was on top of things, but I was surviving in the best way that I could. I didn't have anyone to hold me accountable, and that made it easier for me to fall into that pit of dark depression. I was stressed, overwhelmed, and anxious all the time trying to keep all the balls in the air. I didn't have another choice, so I mentally tried to make it happen, not because I wanted to, but because I had to. I was good at time management, and I applied that to focusing on one thing at a time, which helped me to get my attendance back up.

I'm proud of myself, but I didn't even have time to think about it.

I had to keep moving.

the uphill climb

BEING SO BUSY DIDN'T give me the time to do anything but continue moving. I felt like I was on America's Gladiators on a time clock, doing one task to the next in complete survival mode. It was a coping mechanism, and it helped me to not see how numb I was, and to not feel the deep layers of what was stirring within me.

The one thing I did give up was the normal life of being a teenager. I felt like my teenage years were ripped from me, and I went from being a kid straight to adulthood. At age seventeen, I was living like most kids do once they graduate and leave home. I was going through the motions with school.

I didn't go to parties or sleepovers.

I never went to high school football games, joined in spirit week, or went to movies with friends. And, I didn't go to every school dance.

How am I even going to afford prom?

I'm probably going to be working?

Who would even ask me? I'm never at school.

I was only in the headspace where I went to school, was on time to work, slept, and did it all over again.

I saw the other kids acting like normal teenagers, and it all seems kind of silly to me. I guess that was the point of being a kid. You had time to be silly while others worried about things. I didn't feel like I had that luxury, and I didn't know how to be playful anymore. The last time I had fun was with Grammie years ago before her dementia, and at times with my siblings to make them laugh. But overall, it seems irresponsible to me, but I wished that it didn't. I made a choice being emancipated, but I didn't plan for how lonely I would feel.

Most of the time I was fine. I knew my situation was different than other kids.

I didn't feel happy or sad about it.

It was just the way it was, and I didn'r have much time to dwell on it or to feel sorry for myself. I had moments where I got lonely. It mostly happened late at night when I was alone after work and after my homework was completed—the apartment was dark and still, and the world felt like a vast empty ocean.

The sadness seeped up and spilled over me.

Sometimes it was just lapping waves, and sometimes it was more like a tsunami. Alone in my basement bedroom with only my Walkman for companionship.

I wished that I could be a *normal* girl.

I wished life were easy like it seemed for everyone else, except me. There were nights I wished more than anything that I had a mom, not a mother. I wished that there was someone who would care for me and love me with all their heart. Someone that I could go to and share my concerns, problems, and celebrations. I didn't want to be the strong one, the responsible one, the resourceful one all the time. I just wanted a break and have someone nurture and take care of me for a while.

I often took the interstate 2-15, by the mouth of the canyon to get from school to my place in Sugarhouse. I would have the pedal to the floor, it would go just barely under the speed limit. My car was like "The Little Engine Who Could" as I talked to it saying, "We can do it. You've got this. Here we go."

I would move into the slow lane because people were honking at me. I hoped that I was going to make it up the hill. This felt like my life in general, hoping, trying, pushing up a steep climb.

I still went to Layton almost every weekend to see Dad. These weekends were very important to me, and I knew they were special to him as well. Just as it was hard and lonely for me living by myself, I knew he was sad to be alone, too.

Even when I was backed up with schoolwork or could use the extra shift at work, I found a way to carve out time to see him. When the yellow Subaru breaks down, I rode the bus for an hour and a half to visit.

The weekends where Dad, Trent, and I got together were particularly special. We had a great time together. Dad took us roller skating, bowling, or to the arcade to play pinball. We ate Doritos and donuts and stayed up late watching movies together. Dad and Trent were always silly with each other, and it made me laugh. For those brief weekend moments, I felt like I had a *family*.

The one problem with including Trent on those weekends was that it meant interacting with Mom, but it was worth it to me. Because Dad didn't have a car, it fell on me to get Trent and bring him back home. I always enjoyed our time together in the car, and it was one of the best parts of the weekend. I let my eleven-year-old brother pick out the music to listen to in the car, and we rolled down the windows and jammed out together. I enjoyed the long drive together because that meant more one on one time with him.

Sometimes, I gave him a few extra dollars if I can. I always told him to put the money away in a safe hiding place where Mom couldn't find it.

I knew if she found the money, she'd take it and spend it on cigarettes or junk food for herself. I reminded Trent that no matter what Mom said about me, no matter what *lies* she was telling him, I loved him, and I always would. When we arrived at Mom's house, though, it always got a bit tricky.

When I pulled up, I never went in. I tried to create as little actual contact with Mom as possible.

Yet, she's the queen of drama, so it was impossible to avoid confrontation.

If I was just a few minutes late, she came bustling out and screamed bloody murder at me for being so irresponsible.

Sometimes, though, Mom came out and was very nice to me. This was even worse because it means she wanted money. She knew that I was working. Mom had no shame for hitting me up for money under the guise that she needed it for Trent. I knew the twenty bucks she asked to borrow was really for cigarettes or whatever else she desired that night. I also knew that I'd never see that money again, nor did I even really have any extra money to spare. Yet, I often gave her the money anyway. Why? I had no idea. Maybe I did it to make her go away or because a part of me still wanted to be accepted by her. I wasn't sure. I dreaded these encounters with Mom but dealing with her was so incredibly different. These brief interactions dropping off Trent were nothing compared to how things used to be. Every now and then, I reminded myself of how far I'd come.

I was no longer living with her, and she had no legal hold on me. I needed her for absolutely nothing. Having broken clear, I could now see her for what she was, and it *wasn't* pretty. The difference was now when I saw her, I got angry and upset, but I wasn't scared anymore.

The spell was broken.

I was no longer a hostage inside her dark world.

I was free.

I set my sights on college. I always knew that I was going to go. In fact, my basement apartment was all the way across town in Sugarhouse, while I went to Kearns High because I wanted to rent a place closer to the University of Utah campus to make things easier when I got to college. I always dreamed of going to the University of Utah. Going to college wasn't the "norm" in my family by any means. Only two family members had ever gone before, and neither of them graduated. For me, though, there was no doubt that I'd graduate from all my hard work. I wouldn't accept otherwise, especially after the incident with the school calling Dad. I wanted to be a better person than Mom and I desired to prove that I wouldn't be a high school drop-out like my parents. I wanted to be different, and I needed to make sure that I found my way to college.

Going to college wasn't going to be easy. First, I had to get in, and then I needed to figure out how I was going to pay for it. This was no small feat for someone who struggled just to feed herself. I had saved and worked extra shifts for weeks in order to pay for my payment on my class ring, cap, and gown, as well as my senior pictures. I'd purchased a package with Jostens for all of them, but as it got down to the end, I couldn't make the last two payments. I needed my graduation pictures to place in the invitations, and I had to have a cap and gown to walk with my class. My class ring couldn't be paid for, and I never received it. I was used to paying for it all myself and finding a way to make it happen, so I was devastated that I couldn't finish paying it off.

As with the Schwann's and Ms. Riddley, someone entered my life to help me overcome the challenges before me. I didn't like asking for help and I would rather figure things out on my own because reaching out felt like a failure, but I tried it anyways and turned to Mrs. Gonzalez, my senior year guidance counselor. She invited me into her office, and she listened to my story.

"Wow, you've been through quite a lot for anyone to have to deal with," she said.

I nodded and peered at the floor. "I really want to graduate and go to college."

She patted my hand. "If you really want to graduate you need to kick this in gear. How about you apply for some scholarships?"

I paused, thinking about it. "That sounds great. How do I go about doing that?"

She smiled. "I'd be happy to show you and we can get started on the process."

I have accountability again.

She's taking an interest.

"Can I apply for *all* the scholarships?" I asked, giddy in my seat.

She laughed lightly. "I guess we could, if you'd like."

"I would. I really would."

Mrs. Gonzalez helped me apply for as many scholarships as possible. I didn't even know such potential, and opportunities even existed out there. Under her guidance, I filled out application after application for scholarships that I'd never heard of and never dreamed that I could receive. Mrs. Gonzalez told me that with my grades and extra-curricular activities, I was a strong candidate. That helped me to stay focused and continue to show up for school to make good grades. Because of this, I received a high enough grade point average to join the National Honor Society. She pushed me, encouraged me, and believed in me, even when I didn't believe in myself.

I went in to see her after school when I could to see how things were going with the applications. With her help, I applied for and won scholarships. I won enough scholarships that it was possible to do what I thought was impossible—pay for college tuition. Once again, an influential woman figure taught me how to use my wings when I'd forgotten.

College was in my sights.

I received twenty-three different scholarship offers, and I won an award from Kearns High School for having the most scholarship offers in my graduating class. One of the scholarships that I won was the Papa John's Pizza Scholarship. I got a check for five hundred dollars from Papa John's to use towards my tuition or books AND *all the pizza I can eat*! At the end of the school year, I used the offer to order pizza for all the kids in my anatomy class. It was one big pizza party. For a moment, I went from being nearly invisible to being one of the most popular kids in school.

I was a hero.

For the first time in three years of high school, I felt what I'd be like to be popular. Just as my high school experience was ending, my newfound pizza wealth gave me a brief taste of life as a *regular* teenager.

It was a little too late.

Before I could enjoy it, the year was coming to an end.

all on her own

THE ALARM CLOCK went off and I leaped out of my bed, realizing it was graduation morning.

I smiled.

High School is coming to an end.

I might never see these people from school ever again.

That thought confused me as I wasn't sure how I felt about it. On one hand, I felt joy to move on and to go to college as I had mentally been preparing for it, but I also was nervous about this stage of life ending as it felt like an abandonment for me. Sadness also hit me thinking about how Ms. Riddley wasn't going to be there for graduation. I shook my head trying to ignore it and went to grab the morning newspaper. I put on Dave Matthews Band to help keep my mind off the day ahead and stared at the front page of the *Deseret News*, the local newspaper.

Oh my hell!!

I covered my mouth and gasped.

An article that I was interviewed for at the Tribune looked back at me. I knew that it was coming, but I had idea that it would be published *today!* I was surprised and embarrassed that it was the front-page story in the paper. Everyone would see it. I wanted that, and yet it scared me to have everyone know my story, but I thought it was extremely cool. The article was called "All on Her Own." It knew that it detailed much of what I'd overcome over the last three years while living on my own.

I didn't want to be late and feeling behind brought me anxiety, so I placed the newspaper on the counter, not making time to read the article or think more about its greater meaning. I quickly got dressed, put on mascara and eyeshadow, and did my hair—not something I did often.

I drove myself to the E-Center where graduation was taking place.

The graduating class of 2000 for Kearns High assembled in their gowns in the large convention center. When I arrived, I stood on stage setting up and getting ready to play the Viola with the orchestra. I looked out into the sea of faces, hoping to see Dad and wondering if Mom had a change of heart, and actually showed up. Mom didn't have a job but did have all the time in the world, and she lived *three* miles away. Yet, she told me that she wouldn't be coming to my graduation because "she had no money." I reminded her that the event is FREE. The more I checked for Mom, the more I knew what I had always known. She was not going to be there to support me. I peered at the ground and held my hand. I shouldn't be disappointed. I knew that. Yet, my heart was a funny thing. It still could be broken no matter how much I barricaded it with knowledge, reason, and experience.

I really hoped that Dad would come to see me. He told me that he wouldn't miss my graduation for the world.

Is he going to make it?

He needs to take the day off work.

My mind worried as I waited outside the E-Center for him, knowing that he would have to take multiple buses to get there and that he desperately needed the wages from his job. I didn't want to get my hopes up, but I anticipated his arrival anyways. I scanned the parking lot, but I didn't see him and the more cars that parked, the more my heart sank, but I understood. I looked north at the bus stop. My sinking heart suddenly jumped with joy.

Is that him?

I squinted. Dad stepped off the bus and headed in the direction of where I stood.

Oh, he made it!

I wanted to run to him or do some leaps with how I felt inside, but I smiled and waited for him instead. Dad dressed up for the occasion with slacks, a nice shirt, and a tie. I rarely saw him get ready like that for anything. He looked so handsome. We took a few pictures before we walked in together. Dad took his seat, and I made my way to the stage to play the viola with the orchestra. I felt a nudge as I was walking, and I stared in the direction of where it came from.

"Hey girl. Where are you going?" Jamie asked. "We're walking together, right?"

Wait? She's not mad at me?

I was taken back by her comment as we had lost touch.

Really?!

We had always talked about how we were going to graduate and go to college together.

My heart smiled. "Okay!"

She smiled back and shoulder bumped me. I quickly leaped back into playing a setlist of songs with the orchestra, including Pomp and Circumstance, setting the tone for the people coming in to find their seats for the ceremony.

Shortly after, I got in line to walk with my graduating class to receive my diploma with Jamie. We buried the hatchet with the falling out we had the previous year and walked together just like we promised each other. It felt nice to let go of the frustrations we had toward each other and enter into this new time in our life remembering the good times. It was bittersweet.

After the official ceremony had begun, I was touched that Dad had gone the extra mile to make it because I knew the stretch that it took him to come to my graduation. But, I wasn't surprised as he had always found a way to be there for me. I was thrilled that he watched from the crowd as I accepted my diploma, despite his social anxiety. When my name was called, I was nervous that I was going to fall on my face, but the sense of accomplishment outweighed every other emotion in that moment.

Later, after the ceremony, I hosted a small gathering at my apartment for friends and family. My stomach ached as I busily tried to get the apartment ready so that every detail appeared nice and presentable for whoever decided to come. I hoped that Ms. Riddley would make it and show her support as I hadn't seen her in a while. We had written letters back and forth over the past year and talked occasionally on the phone, and I enjoyed receiving that communication with her. I loved using my Garfield and Lisa Frank stationary to make those special pen pal letters to her. I was excited to show her the article in the newspaper, too. I still hadn't given the newspaper article too much thought, but I wanted to display it. I placed it on a stand on the same table with the cheese and crackers, and meat trays. As guests trickled in, I greeted them and guided them toward the food table that I put together and told them to help themselves. Each time, someone would walk through the door, I got butterflies.

Is Ms. Riddley here?

I went and greeted the guests again, only to feel my energy fall to the floor in a puddle when I didn't see her.

Man, she's not going to come.

No, there's still time for her to make it.

I stared at my watch, realizing she didn't have much time. I went back to the food table and restocked the empty trays with new appetizers. Near the end of the party, I glanced to stare at the door, and there Ms. Riddley stood in the doorway. I smiled and put down the crackers I had in my hand, making my way toward her.

She smiled back at me and gave me a hug. I thanked her for coming.

I gave her a tour of my apartment and we made our way back to the kitchen. I handed her a plate and invited her to grab some appetizers while I went to make sure the rest of the guests were taken care of and had what they needed. When I came back, Ms. Riddley was holding the newspaper article in her hands.

"Tiffany, look how far you've come," she said. "This story is powerful and moving. I'm so proud of you."

I looked in her eyes, and the depth of feeling in Ms. Riddley's face removed me from the moment of rushing around for the first time that day, maybe for the first time in *years*. I stepped away from worrying about my guests for a second and paused to read the article in depth. Seeing all the details of my story written down on paper had a profound effect on me. I started to see the big picture. I could see past all the twists and turns, the endless sleep-deprived days at school, the hard work, the sheer struggle of just getting through the day, and *finally* saw it as parts of a whole. Here, on the day of my graduation, with my personal story surreally splashed on the front page of the local paper, I finally was able to exhale and take pride in what I'd accomplished.

"You should be proud of yourself," Ms. Riddley said.

I nod. "I am proud. I'm so glad you're here. It means a lot to me,"

She peered at me. "I wouldn't have missed it. I'm sorry I'm late."

We continued talking in the kitchen about life, family, her new school, and the next steps toward the future. It reminded me of the conversations we had in the parking lot at Kearns High before she transferred. We had picked right up where we left off and it felt healing.

I didn't want her to go, and I didn't want the day to end, but eventually the party came to a close and everyone left. The future was wide open and so uncertain. I didn't know how to process that. I turned to my journal for clarity and to write the special things that happened on that day so I wouldn't forget. I immediately put my tassel from my graduation cap, on my rearview mirror to decorate my car with a piece of me that I was so proud of.

A few days after graduation, I was surprised when the reporter who wrote the story called my home. She told me that the article had generated an enormous reaction. Since publication, her e-mail box filled with readers' responses to the story. The readers wanted to know how to get in touch with me directly,

and the reporter asked if it would be okay if she forwarded some
of the responses to me.

I agreed.

I was amazed as I went through the responses to the article
as the comments ranged across a broad spectrum. People were
reaching out expressing that I inspired them. Some commented
that they were there if I needed anything, and others offered
to pay for my books in college. I had people who wanted me
to come and speak to various organizations that they were
members of to share my story of overcoming abuse.

There was a man named Dave who was a part of a Rotary
Club, and lived in Millcreek, near the canyon. I had responded
to his message. He had taken me to a rotary club meeting to
introduce me to everyone as the girl that was on the front-page
newspaper article. The group praised me and let me know
that they set aside money for my future. I was taken back
with surprise and gratitude that complete strangers cared and
genuinely wanted to help me.

Other people reached out to tell me their own stories of abuse
and neglect. They felt safe sharing their experiences with me.

Wow! My story really does impact people.

How do I respond to all these people?

I didn't ask for any of this attention, and part of me wanted
it all to go away. I didn't want to serve as a clearinghouse for
abuse stories, either my own or those of others. I'd worked so
hard over the last few years to ensure that my life wouldn't be

defined by the abuse I had endured. Now that I finally arrived at a point where I felt relatively free of the pain and torment that had surrounded me for so long, the last thing I wanted to do was to go back and have my life be about the abuse again. I was no longer the "special circumstance." I was an adult like everyone else and I was ready to move on and start a new life.

The next stop for me was college. I received the scholarships to pay for it and began to prepare for my future. I wanted to sell my banana yellow Subaru to buy a newer model of the Honda Civic. Pre-approval was needed, and I didn't pass. The dealership wouldn't finance me because my credit wasn't there. I didn't have much credit for my age. I went to my credit union and had a sit down with the bank president giving a business proposal on why it would be a good investment to lend me the money to buy this car, despite having established credit. He took a chance on me.

I continued to get an outpouring of responses from my article, primarily from people who had been touched by abuse in some way. I began looking at it from another perspective. By going forward in this way, even though it hadn't been my idea, shed light on the issue and made an impression on their lives. My story had struck a chord in their lives enough for them to step up and do something.

I decided this was my chance to make a difference, and to use my story to influence others to find their light and heal their wounded souls. I couldn't step away.

Multiple invitations came in, inviting me to go and speak to various groups.

When I first read them, I was reluctant.

Will what I say be relevant?

The idea of getting up and telling a bunch of strangers all the intimate details of my life felt like it would be awkward and humiliating. I didn't want to relive the pain. I remembered how empowering it had been when I had gotten up and told my story for the first time at the FCCLA convention.

I went and spoke to Ms. Riddley's class at her new school. Both times with Ms. Riddley, I had been nervous before speaking. It wasn't something that I immediately had any burning desire to do. Yet, once I started, and the nerves melted away a bit, it felt good. It felt *natural*. I expanded beyond telling my own life story and expressed to my audiences how to identify the behavior of people who might have been abused, how to effectively report abuse if they suspected it, and who the best person to speak to about the abuse would be.

Over the summer, I traveled to Moab to speak at an elementary school and a Junior High. I was the speaker for their assembly that day. I also spoke to Junior High classes, Church groups, Girls Sports Teams, and Rotary Clubs. I spoke with adult groups, youth groups, teachers, and entrepreneurs.

Once I moved past the initial reluctance and got more comfortable, I began to handle better what I was trying to say. I started to get a sense of what my story meant both to me and what it could mean to other people as well. No matter what the venue, I told those I was speaking to that if they've experienced abuse, they do *not* have to be a victim. I used my story to encourage them not to become a statistic and share ways to overcome abuse.

I expressed with them the passionate things that had helped me.

"No matter what happens, don't give in to the abuse or sink to the level of those abusing them. Do not repeat the behaviors. Stop it in its tracks. You have the power to stop the cycle."

I encouraged them to reverse their story, become resilient, and empower others to do the same. I tried to present myself as an example that it was a possibility to get through the toughest circumstances—that none of us are prisoners of our situations, and every day is just another chance to turn it all around.

I also started to learn a few tricks to being a good public speaker. Icebreakers or a captivating piece of information helped the audience to engage, and seeing them as people just like me, calmed my nerves.

I got a bag of individually wrapped Lifesaver candies and taped them to a pile of index cards with important contact numbers for reporting abuse. At the end of my talk, I handed out the cards and told everyone to be a "lifesaver" and stop abuse in its tracks.

The most rewarding moments often came after the talks. This was when I got a chance to talk to people one-on-one. Many times, younger people came up to me afterward and talked to me about what they're experiencing in their own lives. Even though they had resources available to them all along in the form of teachers and state workers, these kids would never reach out for help. In fact, they would often deny that any abuse was taking place in their homes when directly approached by a teacher or counselor who suspected something was wrong.

Somehow having someone their own age speaking honestly about the reality of abuse created a comfort level for them. They felt safe coming forward to me and taking that crucial first step towards getting help. Seeing the positive effect that I had on other people's lives was an amazing revelation.

Beyond just surviving— my main focus for years—I began to realize that perhaps this has all happened for a *reason*. I believed that my difficulties may have granted me a strange but wonderful gift that I could use to help people.

It was certainly not the summer I planned for, yet it was *the* summer that shaped my life.

There was no special reason I was able to make it through.

Yet, I did.

If I could do it, they could too!

I made it through the years of being alone stronger than I ever imagined. It hadn't been easy, but all the challenges that I'd overcame gave me the confidence to believe that I could get through anything that came my way.

My life of abuse was OVER.

I felt purpose as I continued to speak and share my message, and the flame within me burned brighter. Getting into my car for my next presentation, I rolled the windows down, and turned the music up. The faster I drove, the more the tassel flew in the wind, and I was ready to take on the next chapter in my life.

My new life had begun.

a flame within

"The spirit that follows the flame, touches your very soul."

THE SUMMER CHANGED ME, as with the Schwann's and then Ms. Riddley. I felt as if that article in *The Deseret News* happened for a reason. I began the summer happy to have made it through high school and relieved to have enough money in scholarships to pay for college. I started the summer convinced that I was going to grow up and be a lawyer. Towards that end, there was no doubt in my mind that at college, I wanted to study law.

Yet, after traveling the state and having so many amazing experiences meeting and speaking to people, I saw the world differently. I felt as if I have somehow uncovered my true purpose. When I enrolled in college in the fall, I'd forgotten all about my plans to be a lawyer.

Instead, I signed up for the University's School of Communication. I wanted to learn as much as I could about how best to connect and help people. It was clear that what I had begun over the summer was the work I'm meant to do. After so many years of living day to day with barely a thought to the future, the path before me seemed clearer. Throughout college, I continued to give talks when I could because it was a passion project for me, but most of my energy was taken up by my studies at school or my part-time job. I wished I could give more talks, but being on an academic scholarship, I needed to focus and maintain grades and classes. I had to have a certain GPA to keep my scholarship. I worked at the bookstore on campus and filed books. I didn't like that much, but that job helped me get discounts on textbooks, and I also was an intern for the honors program. My life was approaching something that almost resembles *normal*. I had roommates in an off-campus duplex, and I had a part-time job that covered my bills.

For the first time, I also had a *real* boyfriend.

One day I came home from school and checked the mailbox on my way in. I began sifting through the mail, finding the envelopes with my name on them, and putting the rest on the counter for the other girls to look through. There was an envelope in my stack from the Salt Lake City Olympic Organizing Committee. Salt Lake City was hosting the 2002 Winter Olympics, and the city bustled with activity, trying to get everything ready. I assumed the letter was part of their fundraising efforts or something. I absently opened the letter, skimming the typed paper.

I paused, holding the paper in my hand.

My attention zeroed in on the letter as I reread it, not quite believing what the words were saying. The letter was an official invitation from the Salt Lake Organizing Committee asking ME if I would like to be one of the official torchbearers for the Olympic Games!!!

I gasped and stared at it in disbelief.

Is this real?

This wasn't something that I applied for and not something that I even knew was possible.

There was a page connected to the letter. "To keep your torch, fill out the form below and send to the return address with a check."

It took me still another read-through to register and believe the words, and to convince myself that the letter was not some joke.

"The person who nominated you, has volunteered to pay the amount for your torch. You're exempt from paying this."

What?

Whoa. I get to keep it?

How is this possible?

Reading the letter for the fourth time, I began to really process what it was explaining. The Olympic Games theme chosen was "*Light the Flame Within*" and individuals across the state who represented this theme were nominated in an anonymous contest. After review, the Olympic

Committee agreed and sent me this letter to ask if I could carry the Olympic Torch.

I smiled.

Are you serious?! This is so exciting!

Who nominated me?

I was curious about who'd take the time to put my name in and recommend me for this huge opportunity.

After I said yes, the official Olympic tracksuit arrived in the mail along with the map for the route I'm going to run.

This is really happening!

I can't believe I'm really doing this.

I'm honored as many famous people will also be carrying the torch on various legs as it travels across the state.

Muhammad Ali himself was going to run the final leg and light the torch in the main Olympic Stadium. These were people who've done great things and inspired many people. I saw myself as just a girl, one of the youngest runners chosen in the state of Utah.

Inside, I wanted to jump up and down, and scream from a mountaintop to the whole world, but I tried my best to take it all in stride and be grateful for how cool this truly was. I was proud, but I didn't want to go around making a big deal out of it. I just wanted to be recognized for strength, resilience, and endurance—the symbol's that the torch meant to me. Deep down, I celebrated quietly with myself feeling incredibly lucky and special knowing that I was chosen and recognizing that not a lot of people could say that they had ran the torch. This was a once in a lifetime opportunity. I knew being part of the Olympic Torch Relay was about being part of something bigger than myself.

I decided to tell Dad and a few others I was close to about the honor. Dad was so excited and told people he worked with all about me and the cool opportunity I was going to be part of. To our surprise, Dad's work bought a torch for me because they didn't know if we would be able to pay for one. I was shocked and humbled that people took an interest in me, but also were watching out for my dad. I had two torches and a lot of people rooting for me as I got prepared for this opportunity of a lifetime. One got placed at Kearns High School and displayed in the halls.

The night before the big day, I took time and care to iron my clothes and make sure there weren't any wrinkles. That act supported me in feeling ready, even though all the butterflies in stomach told me otherwise.

On February 8th 2002, the morning of the Olympic run, my stomach had acted up and all I could think about between nerves and excitement as I got ready to leave was to try and hold it all in.

Please don't get sick.

Not today.

It was a cold and crisp winter day, and the parking lot at Kearns High school was roped off and set-up with a stage for the events of the day. It was across the street from the Olympic Speedskating Oval. A light wind snapped the flags around the stage that had been erected as a way station between legs of the torch's journey. I brought all my gear that they delivered to me weeks previously, and I even bought some white Adidas shoes with three purple lines on them, that matched perfectly with the outfit I was asked to wear. I got to the school an hour early, hoping that my stomach issues would subside by the time I had to run and carry my torch.

"Hi Tiffany. Glad to have you here," a lady said when I arrived at check-in. "You'll have a support runner that will meet you at the stage after you're done getting ready."

I signed in on the clipboard. "Thank you."

"Of course. Follow me," she said. "I'll show you where to get dressed." I smiled and followed behind her into Kearns High School.

This is so weird.

Walking through my old high school, I knew each hall, each staircase, and every corner, like I had never left at all. The random steps in the cafeteria and leading to the Drama room sent waves of nostalgia through me. I often found curiosity in wondering why they were put in that way to begin with. The school always smelled musky when I went to Kearns High, as it was an older school. The scent lingered still as I followed the lady from check-in.

"I'll be right here when you get out."

I nodded and stepped through the door. Moving across the gym to the locker rooms, the smell overwhelmed me with memories, a combo of cleaner, sweat, and rubber. I was standing in the exact spot where I used to play basketball a few years prior.

Once I was in the girl's locker room, I put on my runner's jacket and nylon pants very carefully, making sure that it went on just right. I stood in my purple and white Olympic tracksuit and stared in the mirror.

I smiled.

I've made it.

On the intercom, a countdown for the torch to arrive had begun, and the crowd cheered in the background. My hands shook, and I took a deep breath.

It's time to go.

Embrace the moment.

You've come so far!

I smiled one last time at my reflection and walked out toward the lady who would be escorting me to the stage. Butterflies fluttered in my stomach as I made my way to meet my support runner at the check-in point. Once we were outside, I could feel the energy rise as the radio personality was on stage hyping up the crowd and giving away freebies. When the announcer took a break, the lady at check-in gave me instructions on what was about to happen. She let me know when she would be bringing me on stage and introducing me to the crowd. I attempted to listen as best as I could but stayed grounded trying not to let me anxiety get the best of me.

Before I knew it, my name was being announced and I walked on the stage. Steve Young, the hall of fame quarterback, finished his leg of the procession and ran towards the stage where I was waiting to receive the flame. He dipped his flame into the Olympic cauldron, and I placed my torch into the cauldron next. As soon as the flame lit, I waved at the crowd, and I sobbed uncontrollably. The tears were unexpected as I was overcome with emotion, feeling the power of what the flame in my hand meant to me—inspiration, joy, and awe. Success wasn't the car I drove, clothes I wore, or what I had in my bank account. Success was what I could inspire others to do. I realized in that moment that the spirit that followed the flame, touched my very soul—a symbol that the Olympics represented. That's what I was feeling.

I'm inspiring people.

I'm an inspiration.

The radio personality was saying things on the stage, but it all seemed muffled like hearing through a wind tunnel as my main concern was not to drop my lit torch. I peered up at the flickering blaze. The ancient flame had traveled halfway across the world from Mt. Olympus to be here. It passed from hand to hand, a living testament to the human spirit of strength and endurance.

Now, I was the one entrusted to carry it forward.

My vision blurred.

One step at a time.

I stared at my support runner who was right alongside me. He gave me a thumbs up and I gave him a thumbs up in return. I walked carefully down the steps, and the crowd opened like Moses parting the sea. I started running and began recognizing familiar faces. I saw past teachers and kids who bullied me because of my "special circumstances," all clapping and smiling as if they were SO proud to know me in that moment. These were the same people who thought I'd never amount to anything. Of all places, my leg started in the parking lot of my old high school, across the street from the Olympic Speedskating Oval where Apollo Ono did all his races that year. I said to myself, "You know what, Tiff? You've done Ok."

The moment overwhelmed me as I took stock, realizing how far I'd come.

I have arrived!!

My support runner, continued jogging along next to me, telling me to stay calm.

Keep moving.

I kept running. I felt the wind on my cheeks, and my excitement turned to fuel. I picked up my pace.

"Slow down. Slow down." My support runner yelled.

I took a deep breath. "Okay." I slowed my pace and focused on my heart beating and the feeling of my feet hitting the ground as tears continued to fall down my cheeks. This was what magic felt like.

This moment.

I've made it out.

I have survived.

My light was shining bright!

The Olympic flame had never gone out. It had been part of the games since they began, constantly burning through rain and sun, winter and summer, and in good days and bad. It was a living symbol of the burning spirit inside each one of us—a spirit that may be a small spark at times, and in other moments might be threatened to go out, especially on dark days when we're lost in the storm.

Yet, it never did.

This same flame ignited within me. I somehow kept it lit through all my dark days. I often needed others to help stir the smoldering coals, but I kept it burning. Sometimes it was just a flicker. Yet, it never went out.

On that day, my flame burned with passion for my purpose in this world. My chest filled with an unspeakable joy because I was proud of what I represented being a bearer of the Olympic flame— not just on that day when I ran, but in all the days of my life. Just as others had helped me, I could use my light to help others keep their own flames lit.

I kept running.

I could only imagine what was next.

Life was wide open.

Standing outside our house by the dirt
driveway and lilac bushes.

Riding Bikes with Cousin Reid. Club DRI!!

Posing for one of Mom's photo
sessions outside on the front step.

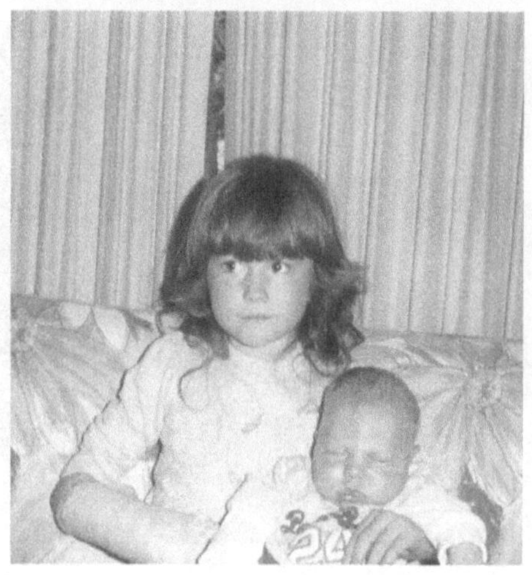

Picture of Troy and me with my
cast on. Age 6.

Grammie and me.

Birthday cake and ice cream for
Troy and me. Age 9.

School picture. Age 13. When Mom
kicked me out.

2002 Olympic Torch Run.

Shirt I had made for SHARE senior
year.

High school graduation with Dad.

Hotline/Support

<u>S.H.A.R.E</u>

Sharing Hope for the Abused through Resilience and Empowerment

S.H.A.R.E was started as a support group for abuse survivors by Tiffany while she was a Junior in high school. S.H.A.R.E is still going strong today and has since evolved into a 501c3 non-profit organization.

S.H.A.R.E is committed to ending all forms abuse and the traumatic effects it has on individual lives, families, communities and nations. Whatever you're going through, there are people who want to help. Whether you are a survivor of past abuse, know of abuse taking place or currently experiencing abuse yourself, you are NOT alone.

Volunteer, donate, sponsor or attend our events! There are many ways you can participate in the movement to end child abuse. Spreading awareness is part of our mission, and we welcome your support.

Please be sure to visit to see what you can do to help in sharing the movement to stop the cycle of abuse one person at a time.

If you or someone you know is in immediate danger call 911

National Child Abuse Hotline   1-800-4-A-CHILD (1-800-422-4453)

National Center Missing & Exploited Children 1-800-843-5678

Teen Dating Violence & Abuse (Love is Respect hotline) 1-866-331-947

National Domestic Violence Hotline   1-800-799-7233

National Sexual Assault Hotline (RAINN) 1-800-656-HOPE (1-800-656-4673)

National Suicide Hotline: 1-800-SUICIDE (1-800-784-2433)

Speak LOUD Podcast

"Speak LOUD even if your voice shakes."

Tiffany started the Speak LOUD Podcast in 2018 as a weekly resource for trauma survivors to come to, Tiffany interviews trauma survivors from across the globe in sharing their stories of triumph and hope focusing not on the abuse itself, rather healthy strategies to overcome that have worked for them. In addition to sharing survivor's stories of triumph and hope, Tiffany also interviews trauma informed care specialists such as: therapists, doctors, counselors as well as various Eastern modalities. The Speak Loud Podcast can be found on most podcast platforms including: Apple Podcasts, Spotify, I-Heart Radio, Stitcher, Buzz Sprout and more. You may also gain access to the weekly episodes by simply going to . Thank you for tuning in!

A Conversation with the Author

What inspired you to write *The Throw Away Girl*?

I wrote The Throw Away Girl because I want survivors to know they are not alone in overcoming abuse. I know it's not an easy road to travel, but I promise you, you can do it. If I did it, you can too. Every day is another chance to turn it all around. It just takes one step toward healing to build momentum toward your dreams and goals. I also wrote my truth, hoping survivors like myself will see that you don't have to use your past as a crutch. You can turn your pain into power as I did. Don't let your past be your whole story, but a chapter in your story. My memoir is my truth. I hope reading it helps you in your journey to your own truth.

What are a few things you've learned about yourself through your journey of resilience?

You can re-write the narrative. I have always tried to view adversity as a challenge, not a trauma. If you're facing overwhelming obstacles, the story you tell yourself about the situation can make a huge difference in how easily you bounce back. If you're willing to do something worthwhile, there's always a risk you'll fail. But by viewing failure as something to learn from, it goes from a dead end to an opportunity for growth.

I don't believe anyone should be expected to just "tough it out." It's about focusing on and prioritizing what you can control and accepting there may be things you can't. What you can control is your perspective and attitude. You can do hard things. It's important to know that change is something we all go through and try to stay positive. I believe resilience is a state of mind. Keep your focus on what you can control and how you will bounce back one day at a time.

Resilience gives us independence; however, on the flip side, a resilient person knows when to ask for help, and they know how valuable a strong support system is. I used to view asking for help as a weakness. Now I realize it takes a village. Ask for help. Don't suffer alone and in silence.

You've had many role models along your path that supported you when you needed it most. What qualities did you admire in them?

One of my greatest role models was my sweet Grammy. She taught me always to value myself and know my worth. She was also known as the "Love you Lady" because she loved everyone around her. I mean EVERYONE! I try to follow in her footsteps and show love to everyone around me—even strangers. It goes with the saying, "Be kind to others. You never know what battles they are fighting."

It's not always easy, but it's worth it. Love is ALWAYS the answer. She taught me that. I've had many role models along the way that taught me many things. I would like to think that I took the best qualities from each one of them and adapted those traits into my own life to make me the thoughtful, resilient, and caring person I am today. I had the chance to be all of them wrapped into one, and I think that's pretty great!

How has the symbol of the torch and "Lighting Your Flame Within," become a daily mantra for you?

I feel that all of us have some flame inside. Sometimes it's a little spark, and you want to give up on life like I once did. Sometimes it's a roaring, raging fire, like when you are passionate about something. Wherever your flame is, it's about doing what you can to feed each other's flame. I feel it's important to do things every day to stoke your own fire but also to fan the flame of one another. Life isn't a solo project. We have the beautiful gift of feeding each other's flame around us every day.

It can be found in the simplest things from listening to someone who had a bad day/experience, spending quality time with a loved one/friend, or telling someone how much you love and appreciate them. The list could go on and on.

If you look at the Olympic Flame, it never goes out. Through all kinds of weather conditions.

I feel we can all be like the resilient Olympic Flame, burning bright and shining our light for others to see no matter our circumstances. Sometimes, others don't feed your flame, and it's all up to you to keep it going. Turn your pain to power. You already have what it takes to survive. Just keep going. Never let your flame go out!

Why do you feel it's important to speak up and speak loud about the epidemic of abuse?

The statistics are freighting that 1 in 4 women and 1 in 5 men suffer some form of abuse. There are so many incredible resources if you're suffering from the effects of abuse. It's never too late. Up until a decade ago, abuse was commonly swept under the societal rug. I love that we live in a time where abuse is more talked about, recognized, and lobbied against. We can call a hotline anonymously to talk to someone or report abuse, listen to a podcast sharing survivors' stories of triumph and hope, or read a memoir like this one.

Seek help from a professional if you feel you're in trouble. There truly are so many resources out there. Find what works for you.

It's about standing in your truth and speaking LOUD, even if your voice shakes. You can do this!

What does *home* mean to you and why is it important?

Only three words describe home for me: Safety, Security, and Stability.

I didn't feel those three words very often when I was little, with all of the bouncing around that I did. As an adult, now that I can control my environment, it's important for me to have these three key things in my home. My home is my sanctuary. A place where I can go to feel protected and safe from the world around me. A place where I can be myself, free from worry or judgment.

The importance of home signals what we think is important in life. You do not have to be wealthy or have a large house to create a space that constantly reminds you of your own deepest values and inspires you to realize them.

To me, home is not a place. It is a feeling. No matter where you call home, the words strike a chord deep inside each of us. You can make a home anywhere, it's about who you are with, not where you are, that really matters.

What are some of your favorite books? What do you love about them?

Shel Silverstein! I really enjoy his books because I used to read them to my Grammy when she was in supervised care or in the hospital. She was a poet, and she taught me to appreciate poetry. Her eyes always lit up when I brought my Shel Silverstein books. She loved them so much, and that was a special memory that continues to make my heart smile!

I've always loved personal de

velopment and self-help books. I remember, even as a teenager heading to the Self-Help section of any bookstore. I always enjoyed reading about different techniques and strategies to better myself. I think they played a huge role in my perspective on what happened to me growing up.

Recently, I have really been into authors such as Michael Singer, Eckhart Tolle, and Joe Dispenza. I have found so much relief and solace in reading spiritual books from these authors.

What advice can you share on how we can better support kids and teens going through forms of abuse?

My number one piece of advice is to listen. I know, personally, how impactful having someone listen to me was in my journey of healing and seeking help. I'm talking about active listening. When I felt truly heard by someone, the more I opened up about what was truly going on. That also goes in conjunction with trust. Having someone that I trusted to listen to me was key. When that person comes to you, remain calm. Reassure them that they did nothing wrong. It is not their fault, and they will not be punished. Tell them you believe them and that you're glad they told you. Offer comfort. Let them know you will help. Ensure both the safety of you and them. Tell them you can't keep this information secret (in many states, it is the law). Report the abuse to the authorities immediately. Be there for them every step of the way through the process of recovery.

Acknowledgements

So many people have been instrumental in my journey of writing this book. It's hard to know where to even begin.

First, a special thank you to my sweet Grammie for being my Earth angel. You always saw the best in me and showed me what it meant to be loved unconditionally. You had a way of making me feel so special and played such a tremendous role in the woman I am today. There is not a day that goes by that I don't miss and think of you. You are always in my heart. "I love you a bushel and a peck and a hug around the neck."

I would like to honor Dan Clark for seeing what I didn't see in myself 22 years ago and encouraging me to write a book about my life. My life was forever changed the day I met you. Thank you- You inspire me!

To my beautiful sister, you've been bragging about me writing this book for YEARS to anyone who would listen. I can't believe it is finally here! We have been through so much together, but I wouldn't change it for the world. I am incredibly proud of you and the woman you are today. Thank you for your love and unwavering support. You are so special to me. I love you to the moon and back!

Enormous gratitude goes to my editor, dear friend, and literary maven, Lauri Schoenfeld. I would truly not have made it this far in publishing my book without your guidance. I'm confident it would probably still be sitting in a file somewhere on my computer if it wasn't for your dedication and patience. Thank you for holding space for me and making me feel incredibly supported in this wild journey to the finish line.

My appreciation goes out to Brent Palmer for being such a catalyst in the success of S.H.A.R.E and my motivational speaking early on. You believed in me more than I believed in myself most times. Thank you for helping me find places to share my message and pushing me outside my comfort zone.

To the Schwab family, thank you for opening your home and providing me with a safe place to land during one of the most difficult times in my life. You took me in as your own and provided me a true sense of home, showing me what it felt like to be a part of a family like I had never known before.

A special thank you to Amy for picking up the phone that day. Your friendship kept me going. Without you, I may not have been here to write and publish this book today.

To Ms. Eardley, thank you for making me feel seen and heard at a time of my life when I felt invisible. Your presence and faith in my resilience meant more than you will ever know or understand.

To my high school guidance counselor Cheri Gonzales, thank you for your gentle nudges to keep me going senior year. You sent the rescue boat when I felt like I was drowning. I will never forget that.

A huge thank you to Shirley. You've been my biggest fan, cheering me on through thick and thin. Thank you so much for pushing me to get my story out there, especially on days I felt like throwing in the towel. You are an amazing woman. I am so glad our paths reconnected. I love you mucho, mucho!

Deepest gratitude goes to the beta readers: Kate Rinlisbacher, Lark Dean Galley, Bryce Prescott, Rebecca Lamoreaux, Cindy Bennett, and Kathy Jenkins Oveson. Thank you for volunteering your time and effort. The advice and criticism you gave truly helped weave the pieces of this memoir together into the beautiful final version it is today.

To my dad, you were broken and empty and couldn't give me what you didn't have. You were a child raising a child the best way you knew how. Thank you for always showing up for me, even when it meant taking a long way to get there. I know you never meant to hurt me.

I also want to thank the countless friends and family who cheered me on in my journey to getting this book done through the years. I am the luckiest girl in the world for having your endless support—much love and gratitude to each of you. There are too many of you to name. You know who you are.

Finally, thank you, the reader, for your support in purchasing this book. I hope it helps feed your flame. May you always know; you are never alone, you matter, you can do hard things, and you are ALWAYS ENOUGH! Stand in your truth and keep on shining your light!

Meet Tiffany Barnes

TIFFANY CURRENTLY RESIDES in Salt Lake City, Utah, with her two dogs, Max and Rocco, and her cat, Sasha. She's following her passion for helping others overcome abuse through her work as an author, a host of the Speak Loud Podcast, and the founder of S.H.A.R.E- Sharing Hope for the Abused through Resilience and Empowerment, a 501c3 created by survivors for survivors.

Tiffany's hobbies include cycling, bowling, paddle boarding, and public speaking. She enjoys spending time with her friends and family, riding her bike outdoors, and doing what she can to be a lighthouse to others. Tiffany has made it her mission to help others to create real change, one person at a time. Her motto is "It's the START that STOPS you." Through her message, Tiffany encourages people to begin their journey of resilience and empowerment from adverse circumstances one step at a time.

Visit her at www.thethrowawaygirl.com.

To learn more about S.H.A.R.E and how you can help to reverse the cycle of abuse one person at a time visit www.sharethemovement.org.

To tune into her podcast sharing stories of triumph and hope for trauma survivors visit www.speakloudpodcast.com.